Game for Gourmets

with seasonal starters and puddings

Published by RMC Brainwave

A Game-to-Eat publication for
The Countryside Alliance
The Old Town Hall
367 Kennington Road
London SE11 4PT

First published 2007

ISBN 978-0-9556128-0-0

Game for Gourmets

Edited by
Chris Catlin and Iain Middleton

Photographed by
Richard Faulks

Designed and produced by
Mik Baines

Printed in England by
Gildenburgh Ltd, Peterborough

Game is wild, natural and full of flavour, all of which makes it a great alternative to our everyday fare.

It's no wonder chefs enthuse about the many variations they can offer on their restaurant menus.

Game lovers are spoilt for choice - a wide variety is readily available from the British countryside.

What's more, game is low in cholesterol and high in protein, making it one of the healthiest kinds of meat available.

 **Game for Gourmets** is sponsored by the Countryside Alliance's **Game-to-Eat** campaign.

Game for Gourmets
Exciting new ways of cooking with game

Four of Britain's acclaimed gastropub chefs have selected their most popular game dishes, seasonal starters and puddings - and show how you can prepare them quickly and easily at home.

Game for Gourmets offers an innovative menu of natural, wild game from the British countryside - including pheasant, partridge, venison, grouse, duck, pigeon and rabbit.

Whatever the occasion - mid-week supper, dinner party or quiet night in with someone special - you'll find the right recipe in this new cook book.

A quartet of chefs

All our chefs are passionate about local produce, especially game. They run busy kitchens, where freshness is vital and where every minute counts. Many of the dishes they have selected can be cooked and served in less than half an hour – though for some you'll need to prepare one or two ingredients in advance.

Mark Gough
Tollemache Arms, Buckminster, Leics

Proprietor and chef of a gastropub set in the heart of a long established shooting estate. Formerly chef at the Restaurant Pierre Orsi, Lyons; Raymond Blanc's Le Manoir aux Quat'Saisons, Oxford; Hambleton Hall, Rutland; and, from 1997 to 2004, head chef at Hart's, Nottingham.

Sean Hope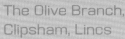
The Olive Branch,
Clipsham, Lincs

Sean has been chef at The Olive Branch since 1999, when he and his associates bought the property with the aim of revitalising a village pub. Previously Sean was second chef at Hambleton Hall, near Oakham, after working at Longueville Manor in Jersey, The Feathers in Woodstock, and the Criterion in London. Trained at Stamford College, he is a firm believer in making the most of local produce.

David Lem
Houghton's at The Pear Tree
Woodhouse Eaves, Leics

David opened his own restaurant in 2006 after two years as head chef at The Queen's Head, in the nearby village of Belton. He was head chef at The Aquarium, St Katherine's Dock, London, and at Bentley's seafood restaurant on Piccadilly. Earlier he worked at The Canteen, Chelsea Harbour, where he cooked the occasional private dinner for its co-owner, film star Michael Caine.

Neil Dowson
The Lawns,
Holt, Norfolk

Neil Dowson took over at The Lawns after five years at The Victoria in Holkham, where he also looked after private functions for the Earl and Countess of Leicester. Before that Neil was head chef at the Loch Torridon Hotel in Scotland and second chef at The Savoy in London, The Vineyard at Stockcross in Berkshire and the Fleur de Sel in Haslemere, Surrey.

Contents

Starters

Cooking times and quantities
Each recipe serves four unless otherwise stated. All cooking times in this book are a guide. They can vary according to the size or age of the gamebird or the type of oven. Allow one gamebird per person, apart from pheasant and mallard which should serve two.

Gamekeepers' broth

This is a great winter warmer - and always popular with the guns, gamekeepers and everyone else out shooting on a frosty day.

Preheat oven to 200°C. Roast the carcasses in a well-oiled roasting tin until golden brown, then place in a stockpot with the chopped onion and carrot, tomato purée, thyme and bay leaves.

Cover with water and simmer with the lid on for about an hour, drain the stock through a fine sieve and reduce by half to strengthen the flavour.

Cook the pearl barley in salted water until tender, drain, refresh in cold water and keep to one side.

To finish the soup, heat the game stock and add the carrot, potato, leek and celery. Simmer for eight to ten minutes until tender, add pearl barley and chopped game and re-heat for two minutes.

Serve with warm, crusty bread.

Ingredients
Serves four

Stock
2 game bird carcasses
1 tbsp vegetable oil
1 onion
1 large carrot
1 tbsp tomato purée
2 bay leaves
1 sprig of thyme

Broth
3 large carrots, peeled and diced
2 large potatoes, peeled and diced
2 leeks, diced
2 sticks of celery, diced
100g pearl barley, soaked for 24 hours
200g chopped breast or leg meat (leftovers)

Pigeon salad with wild mushrooms and Madeira vinaigrette

Wood pigeons are a great fast food. Unlike some game, they don't require hanging. Once plucked, they can be cooked and eaten almost straight away.

For the Madeira dressing, heat the Madeira in a pan until it is reduced by half, add the white wine vinegar and stir in the olive oil. Season with a little salt and pepper. Set aside.

Pick over and wash the wild mushrooms, using a nail brush to remove any bits of dirt. Slice the larger mushrooms.

Skin the pigeon breasts and carve them off the bone. Heat a frying pan with a little olive oil, season the pigeon breasts with salt and pepper and fry the breasts for 2 to 3 minutes each side. Remove from the pan, leave to rest and keep warm.

In the same pan, add another splash of oil and fry the chopped shallots, then the mushrooms and cook for 2 minutes, season with salt and pepper

Dress the salad leaves with the Madeira dressing, and place on a plate. Spoon the mushrooms over the salad and slice the pigeon and lay it on top.

Ingredients
Serves four

150ml Madeira
30ml white wine vinegar
200ml olive oil
Salt and pepper
Breasts of 4 pigeons (keep the carcasses for stock)
2 shallots, peeled and finely chopped
400g of various wild mushrooms
4 handfuls of your favourite salad leaves

Pigeon on toast

Provided you have the onion marmalade ready in advance, this is a quick and extremely tasty starter or snack.

Onion Marmalade Slice onions finely and 'sweat' in a frying pan with a knob of butter and a pinch each of salt, pepper and sugar. Fry until translucent, move the onions to one side and use white wine or sherry vinegar to deglaze the pan.

Season with a little orange juice and reduce the liquor by half. Stir the onions back in and set aside to cool if you're keeping it in the fridge for later. Otherwise keep warm until serving.

If you are not in a hurry, marinate the pigeon breasts in red wine in the fridge overnight to enhance the flavour and keep them moist.

Red Wine Sauce Mix and heat port and red wine in a saucepan, reduce by half, then add the stock. Reduce again so the sauce is just thick enough to 'coat' the pigeon breasts.

Heat vegetable oil in a frying pan. Pat the pigeon breasts dry with kitchen paper, season with salt and pepper and sear for 2 to 3 minutes each side. Rest in a warm place but away from the heat.

Drizzle the slices of bread with olive oil and toast lightly under a grill. Before serving spread with onion marmalade.

Use wine sauce together with olive oil and balsamic vinegar to dress the dish.

Serve with a green salad of rocket, pine nuts and cos lettuce with a light vinaigrette - a combination of groundnut oil, white wine vinegar (ratio four-to-one) with salt and pepper.

Ingredients
Serves two

Onion Marmalade
2 medium onions
(red, if preferred)
A knob of butter
Salt, pepper and sugar
2 tbsps white wine or sherry vinegar
Splash of fresh orange juice

Breasts of 2 pigeons
2 glasses (300 ml) red wine
Salt and pepper
1 tbsp vegetable oil
2 thick slices of bread
2 tbsps olive oil

Red wine sauce and dressing
1 glass (150 ml) red wine
1/2 glass of port
200 ml chicken stock
2 tsps olive oil
1 tsp balsamic vinegar

Salad
40g rocket salad
20g cos lettuce
2 tsps toasted pine nuts
1 tbsp groundnut oil
1 tsp white wine vinegar

Pigeon breasts with pea risotto

Peafields are a magnet for hungry pigeons, so perhaps it's no coincidence that pea risotto combines so well with seared pigeon breasts.

Add whipping cream to a saucepan, warm through and add the peas. Heat through until the peas are tender, then allow to cool before mashing coarsely in a blender. Set aside.

For the risotto heat the butter until frothing in a heavy frying pan. Add a crushed garlic clove and a sprig of thyme but no salt or pepper just yet. Add rice and stir, adding about half a cup of stock to start the process.

Keep stirring and add another half cup as the first evaporates. Continue adding stock or water gradually until the risotto is al dente (slightly firm). This takes at least 15 minutes. Next, add the grated parmesan and prunes.

Fry pigeon breasts in a well-oiled frying pan with salt and pepper, chopped thyme, a quarter clove of garlic and a knob of butter. About 2 to 3 minutes each side will be enough. Use the pan juices cleared with a splash of orange juice to coat the pigeon breasts before resting them.

Now stir the mashed peas into the risotto, add finely chopped chives, a little more parmesan, perhaps some lemon juice plus a pinch of cayenne pepper and salt. Stir in finely chopped mint and chives before serving.

Crostini of seared pigeon breast with kumquat chutney

Here's a Mediterranean style snack or starter that is really light and easy to prepare - and wood pigeon is available all year round.

Game needs a contrasting touch of sweetness, so this dish features a chutney made by combining kumquats with sugar and Cointreau. The mixture is heated and stirred in a pan over a medium heat until the kumquats soften and the chutney thickens.

For the crostini halve bread rolls, drizzle with olive oil and toast in an oven preheated to 200°C.

Brown the pigeon breasts in vegetable oil and butter in a hot, heavy bottomed pan. This takes two to three minutes each side, less if you like your meat rare. Remove from pan, dab off excess oil with kitchen paper and allow to rest.

For the sweet balsamic dressing, simmer balsamic vinegar with port, red wine and sugar. Add cinnamon bark, a clove and orange zest. Render down to a syrupy consistency.

Place the pigeon breasts on rocket salad on top of the crostini and decorate as shown.

Ingredients
Serves four

Chutney
20 kumquats
150g sugar
50ml Cointreau

4 pigeon breasts
1 tbsp olive oil
1 tbsp vegetable oil
50g butter
2 medium bread rolls
100g or 4 small handfuls rocket salad

Sweet balsamic dressing
125ml balsamic vinegar
25ml port
25ml red wine
50g sugar
1/2 stick cinnamon bark
1 clove
Pinch of orange zest

Pigeon bruschetta with pâté de foie gras

Once regarded as plain and simple country fare, wood pigeon takes on a touch of luxury with the addition of goose liver pâté.

Put the port, sugar and orange juice and zest in a pan and reduce to a syrupy consistency over a gentle heat. Set aside.

Heat a heavy pan with a teaspoonful of vegetable oil until it is searing hot. Season the pigeon breast fillets with salt and pepper and seal on each side for two minutes or so. This will cook the pigeon to rare.

If you like it less rare, increase the cooking time accordingly. Set aside and allow to rest.

Drain off any excess oil from the pan, return to a high heat and once it starts to smoke take four slices of foie gras and seal for about 20 seconds only on each side. The foie gras will release plenty of fat to provide a nice caramel coating so it should not stick to the pan.

Toast four thick triangles of bread. Pain d'épices can usually be bought from a delicatessen. Alternatively you can use toasted fruit loaf or walnut and prune bread.

Assemble the dish with the toast triangle as a base. Spread with red onion marmalade. Next, slice each pigeon breast into two and place on the bread. Top with sliced foie gras.

Heat port and orange sauce and drizzle over the pigeon breasts and plate.

Ingredients
Serves four

Breasts of 2 pigeons
300g pâté de foie gras
2 slices pain d'épices,
halved diagonally
4 small glasses (400 ml)
of port
Juice and zest of 2
oranges
2 tbsps sugar
2 tsps vegetable oil
Salt and pepper
4 tbsps red onion
marmalade
(recipe, page 21)

Game terrine with quince purée

A wonderful terrine, either for a dinner starter or as a useful standby in the fridge. The recipe may seem time consuming - but it is certainly worth the effort.

Start with the quince purée. Peel and chop the quinces, removing the core and pips. Place in a small pan and fill with just enough water to cover the fruit. Then add a knob of butter and about 1 tbsp of sugar. Simmer until tender, then purée in a blender.

Grease the inside of the terrine mould and line with the streaky bacon, leaving an overhang that can be folded back over the top.

Fry the onion until soft. When cold, add the onion to the minced game and pork in a large bowl, then add chopped livers and herbs . Add brandy, port, chopped hazelnuts and seasoning. Mix well.

Place a layer of the mince mix in the bottom of the mould, pressing it right into the corners. Place game pieces on top of the mince, then add another layer of mince, filling in the gaps as you go.

Continue until the top of the meat and mince sits just above the rim of the mould. Lay overhanging bacon back across the top, cover with a piece of buttered foil and put a lid on the mould. Place in a deep baking tray containing enough warm water to reach about half way up the mould.

Cook in a pre-heated oven at 180°C for about one hour 20 minutes. The terrine is done when it has shrunk a little from the side of the mould and the juices are clear, not pink. Remove the tray from the oven and press the mould down with a weighted chopping board.

When cold, refrigerate for 24 hours before serving with quince purée, green salad and toast.

Ingredients
Serves 10 to 12

One standard terrine mould (a 2lb / 1kg loaf tin would work just as well)
2 quinces
Cold water
1 tbsp caster sugar
Knob of butter
500g thinly sliced streaky bacon
1 large white onion, finely chopped
500g minced game
300g minced pork
100g chopped livers, game or chicken
5 sage leaves
1 large sprig of thyme
2 tbsps brandy
1 tablespoon of port
50g hazelnuts, peeled and chopped
15 turns of a pepper mill
25g sea salt
250g various game pieces, boned and trimmed, rabbit, pheasant or venison
Green salad

Peppered hare loin
with goat's cheese

Quick and versatile, this recipe highlights the delicate flavour of the hare - but it is just as tasty when used for duck or pigeon breast.

Coat the loin with crushed black and white peppercorns and crushed juniper berries. The peppered loin can be wrapped in cling film and kept in the fridge until needed for cooking.

Sear the loin briskly in a hot, well oiled frying pan, adding chopped rosemary for flavouring. Seal for two minutes each side. Set aside to rest.

Dress a seasonal salad with a light vinaigrette of the groundnut oil and white wine vinegar - mixed in a ratio of four-to-one - plus salt and pepper to taste.

Halve the goat's cheese, splash with balsamic vinegar and sear briefly under the grill. Alternatively, bake the cheese in a warm oven for a couple of minutes to soften, then sear with a blow torch.

Place the cheese on a bed of the salad, slice the hare loin thinly and lengthways and arrange round the cheese.

Use a splash or two of olive oil and balsamic vinegar to clear the pan juices and add a few of the crushed peppercorns and a little chopped rosemary to the jus. Stir and drizzle over the dish to finish.

Ingredients
Serves two

Loin of one hare
(half per portion)
Crushed black and white peppercorns
2 or 3 juniper berries
Sprig of fresh rosemary, finely chopped
2 handfuls of seasonal salad
1 tbsp groundnut oil
1 tsp white wine vinegar
Salt and pepper
125g soft-rind goat's cheese
2 tsps balsamic vinegar
1 tbsp olive oil

Seared hare loin with figs steeped in mulled wine

In areas with a stable hare population February is usually the month for organised hare shoots. Keep a reserve of hare joints in the deep freeze and you can enjoy this hearty dish at any time of the year.

Bring wine and honey to the boil and add the figs. If the figs are not ripe they can be cooked briefly in the mulled wine until they have softened slightly. Allow the wine and figs to cool. If prepared in advance, seal in a sterilised Kilner jar or similar airtight container and refrigerate until needed.

Seal the hare loin in a hot frying pan with olive oil. About two minutes each side should do the trick. Deglaze the pan with a splash of fresh orange juice. Coat the hare loin with the pan juices and set aside to rest.

Dress the rocket with groundnut oil and mix with toasted pine nuts and avocado. Season with salt and pepper and a splash of lemon juice.

Slice the hare loin lengthways at an angle to make the slices as large as possible and arrange on the plate with the salad and halved figs.

Ingredients
Serves four

Two hare fillets
(removed from the
saddle and the loin)
6 fresh figs
1/2 bottle red wine
1 tbsp honey
2 tbsps olive oil
1 tbsp fresh orange juice
100g rocket salad
2 tbsps groundnut oil
25g toasted pine nuts
1 avocado, sliced
1 tsp lemon juice
Salt and pepper

Smoked venison with fig tarts

Delicious country fare with a touch of showbiz... this dish is all about presentation. A little time spent assembling each portion will create a stunning visual effect.

Place the pitted cherries in a large pan and sprinkle with sugar, red wine vinegar and balsamic. Then cook them down gently until tender while still retaining their shape.

Make a criss-cross cut in the top of the figs, splash with sugar and balsamic vinegar and bake on a tray at 200°C for about five minutes until soft.

For each pastry case, cut three-inch (7cm) squares of filo pastry. Butter one layer and add another buttered layer on top until the square consists of four layers. Shape round a buttered egg cup and bake in a hot oven at 200°C until golden (about five minutes).

Roll slices of smoked loin of venison into rose shapes. For each portion these are set on top of three separate dessertspoonfuls of onion marmalade.

Once the pastry baskets have cooled add the figs and assemble the plate as shown with the cherries.

12 thin slices smoked venison
150g red onion marmalade (double the recipe on page 21)

Pickled cherries
40 cherries, pitted
100g sugar
50ml red wine vinegar
50ml balsamic vinegar

Tarts
4 small fresh figs
4 large sheets filo pastry
50g melted butter

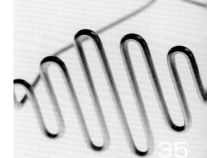

Venison tartare, salad leaves and fried quails' eggs

Not surprisingly it was a cook from the Scottish Highlands who developed this variation on the classic steak tartare. You can easily vary the ingredients and quantities to suit your own taste.

Chop the venison loin as finely as you can. You can use a food processor, but the texture is better if you chop it. Then add as many of all the other ingredients as you prefer (listed quantities are only a guide).

If you like it spicy, add more Tabasco. If you like it piquant, increase the amount of capers - it's up to you.

Once that's done, shape the mixture into small patties.

Dress the salad leaves with some vinaigrette.

Fry the quails' eggs in sunflower oil and sit one on top of each tartare. Serve as shown.

Ingredients

Serves four
600g loin of venison, trimmed of all fat and sinew
4 shallots, finely chopped
1 tsp capers, roughly chopped
4 small gherkins, roughly chopped
2 tbsps flat leaf parsley, chopped
Worcestershire sauce
Tabasco sauce
Salt
Freshly ground black pepper
4 handfuls various salad leaves, washed
Vinaigrette
(recipe, page 57)
4 quails' eggs
1 tsp sunflower oil for frying eggs

Wigeon with pink grapefruit and rocket salad

For those who like the duck and orange theme this makes a perfect light meal for warmer autumn days.

Skin pink grapefruit and cut into segments, saving the juice. Slice grapefruit skin into marmalade-style strips and blanch for about ten minutes in cold water brought slowly to the boil.

Allow water to cool, add a tablespoonful of sugar and bring to the boil again. Allow to cool, drain and set the grapefruit strips aside.

Carve duck breasts off the bone. Add a little vegetable oil to a heavy pan over a medium heat and, once the oil is hot, seal the breasts skin side down for up to 3 minutes. Remove from heat and take off the skin.

Return duck to the heated pan, this time add butter and reseal on both sides. This takes two to three minutes each side. Remove from heat and set aside to rest.

Arrange grapefruit segments on a plate. Add rocket seasoned with salt and pepper, spring onion and a pinch of chives. Dress with balsamic vinaigrette made from olive oil and balsamic. Save a spoonful for the next step.

Carve the duck into strips and place on the salad bed. Season with salt, pepper and the saved grapefruit juice. Decorate with shreds of grapefruit skin and drizzle with remaining balsamic vinaigrette.

Ingredients
Serves two
1 wigeon, dressed
2 tbsps vegetable oil
25g butter
1 pink grapefruit
1 tbsp sugar
50g rocket
1 spring onion, chopped
Pinch of chopped chives
Salt and pepper
2 tbsps olive oil
1 tbsp aged balsamic vinegar

Teal with pickled walnuts and baby spinach

Teal is our smallest quarry duck and, according to some wildfowling and shooting enthusiasts, it's also the tastiest. In this dish walnuts and spinach set off the duck's natural flavour.

Heat vegetable oil and butter in a heavy-bottomed pan with one crushed clove of garlic and a sprig of thyme.

Over medium heat seal the duck for about one-and-a-half minutes on each leg side, then each breast side. Finally place the duck on its back in the pan and roast in a preheated oven at 200°C for four minutes.

Rest for two minutes or more before carving off the breasts and legs. Season with salt and pepper plus a splash of orange juice to taste. Any surplus duck skin can be cut into strips and used as a garnish (optional).

Slice pickled walnuts and set out on a plate. Season baby spinach leaves with peanut oil, a splash of lemon juice, salt and pepper and make a bed for the teal.

Place the teal on top of the spinach as shown and decorate the dish with a vinaigrette made from olive oil and balsamic.

Ingredients
Serves two
Two teal, dressed
2 tbsps vegetable oil
25g butter
1 clove garlic
Sprig of thyme
Salt and pepper
Fresh orange juice
4 pickled walnuts
50g baby spinach leaves
1 tbsp peanut oil
Juice of 1/2 lemon
2 tbsps olive oil
1 tbsp aged balsamic vinegar

Cream of wild mushroom soup with Stilton toast

Be warned, this is a hearty starter! A light meal in itself, this soup and cheese combination is perfect on a cold day.

Start by frying the chopped thyme, garlic and onion in vegetable oil until the onion is translucent. Add field mushrooms and 'sweat' them down for a minute or two. Pour in the Madeira and light with a match to flame the pan.

Cover the mushrooms with chicken stock, or vegetable stock if you prefer. Cook for a maximum of 10 minutes over a low to medium heat. Remember that the more you cook, the more flavour you lose. You may find the mushrooms are tender after just five minutes.

As soon as they are done, allow to cool, transfer to a blender and blend until smooth. Return the mix to the pan, add double cream, salt and pepper, and stir in. Heat through – but be careful not to boil - before serving.

To garnish, fry a small quantity of sliced wild mushrooms until crisp. We've used chanterelle and trumpet mushrooms, but you can use whatever are available. Float these on the surface of the soup and drizzle round them a couple of rings of double extra virgin olive oil.

Bake the Stilton on long slices of rye bread in an oven at 200°C until it is starting to melt. Serve alongside as shown.

Ingredients

Serves four

1kg field mushrooms, chopped

1 large onion

2 cloves garlic

2 sprigs thyme

2 tbsps vegetable oil

50ml Madeira

1 litre chicken stock

200ml double cream

Salt and pepper

6 small wild mushrooms

2 tbsps double extra virgin olive oil

200g Stilton cheese

1 large loaf rye bread

Crispy goat's cheese parcels, fresh figs, salad and walnut dressing

This recipe complements the subtle flavours of the goat's cheese. It's also a dish for all seasons - you just change the fruit.

Layer two large sheets of filo pastry, brushed in between with melted butter. Cut into 16 squares, each 4in / 10cm square. Place a piece of goat's cheese in the centre of each square and sprinkle with cracked black pepper.

Bring all corners together and crimp tightly to seal, making a purse shape.

Preheat oven to 190°C and bake pastry parcels for about 10 minutes until golden brown. Season parcels with celery salt.

For the walnut dressing, place the walnuts and other ingredients except oil in a blender and blitz for ten seconds. Gradually add olive oil and walnut oil and season with salt and pepper. If the dressing starts to look a little thick, thin down with a teaspoon of warm water.

Toss the salad ingredients in the walnut dressing and divide onto four plates. Arrange four crispy goat's cheese parcels around each salad plate with a fresh fig cut into four.

Ingredients
Serves four

Parcels
2 soft-sided 100g goat's cheeses, each cut into eight
2 large sheets filo pastry
100g butter
Cracked black pepper
Celery salt

Walnut dressing
8 roasted walnuts
1 egg yolk
1 tsp honey
1 tsp grain mustard
1 tsp cider vinegar
100 ml olive oil
100 ml walnut oil

Salad
1 package mixed salad leaves
1 red onion, finely chopped
6 roasted walnuts
1 tsp chopped herb fennel
4 fresh figs

Mushroom and Lincolnshire Poacher rarebit

This snack is no fuss to prepare and makes a refined first course or a really wholesome brunch.

Melt butter in a thick bottomed saucepan. Add flour to form a roux and stir well with a wooden spoon until it begins to come away from the side of pan. Gradually add milk, mixing thoroughly to obtain a smooth consistency. Cook out the sauce for 5 to 10 minutes before adding Lincolnshire Poacher cheese, mustard and Worcestershire sauce.

Remove pan from heat and stir in egg yolks. Season to taste, cover and leave to cool.

Mushrooms Heat frying pan, drizzle with olive oil and add a knob of butter. Sweat off a little chopped onion, add a good handful of sliced blewitt mushrooms – alternatively you could try oyster, ceps, girolles or shitake mushrooms - and sauté until golden brown. Season to taste, finish with a squeeze of lemon juice and chopped tarragon.

Cut four slices of bread, nice and chunky, and toast. Granary or pumpkin seed bread is ideal if you can get it. Place pieces of toast on an oven tray and scatter with the sautéd mushrooms.

Spread the rarebit mixture liberally over the mushrooms and place under a hot grill until golden brown.

Chef's tip Serve with either crispy smoked streaky bacon or a homemade fruit chutney.

Ingredients
Serves four

Rarebit
50g unsalted butter
50g plain flour
300 ml milk
150g Lincolnshire Poacher cheese, grated
(Mature Cheddar is a good substitute)
4 thick slices of granary bread
1 tsp English mustard
1 tsp Worcestershire sauce
2 egg yolks

Mushrooms
200g blewitts or other mushrooms
1 tbsp olive oil
25g butter
1 small onion, chopped
Juice of 1/2 lemon
1 tsp chopped tarragon
Salt and pepper

Baked hazelnut goat's cheese with pears poached in red wine

Cooking goat's cheese tends to soften any of its natural bitterness. The combination with hazelnuts strikes a perfect balance - and it's just as good with Mediterranean vegetables.

Peel the pears and poach whole until tender in red wine flavoured with cinnamon, star anise and orange zest. Remove the pears, slice lengthways into quarters and core. Reduce the liquor to thicken and set aside.

Chop hazelnuts to breadcrumb consistency in a blender, saving a few whole ones as decoration. Dip each half goat's cheese in egg white, then roll in hazelnut coating. Cover the cheese well. Bake at 200°C until softened and heated through (about 15 minutes).

Use olive oil and a little of the reduced pear liquor to dress the salad. Here mustard leaves are used for the salad, but rocket or watercress would be just as good.

For the base, toast rounds of brioche in a pan with just a drop or two of olive oil on each side. Assemble the plate with a half a toasted cheese on each round of brioche, quartered pears, dressed salad and whole hazelnuts.

Ingredients
Serves four

Poached pears
2 Comice or Williams pears
1 stick cinnamon
1 star anise
Zest of 1 orange
1/2 bottle red wine
2 soft-rind, goat's cheeses (each 100g), sliced in half
1 egg white, beaten
200g hazelnuts, toasted
1 handful salad leaves (mustard leaf, rocket or watercress)
4 large slices of brioche
2 tbsps olive oil

Partridge

The partridge season starts in September, a month before pheasant shooting. That means fresh partridges are available for the table for five months, until the end of January.

Chefs differ on whether they require hanging - but a brace will keep for several days in a cool place before they're needed in the kitchen.

Grey or English partridges are nothing like as common these days as French or redleg partridges, which will generally be the variety offered for sale.

Pheasant

There are wild pheasants in many parts of Britain - the species is said to have been introduced by the Romans - and their numbers are vastly increased each year by birds that are reared and released for game shoots.

Pheasant shooting starts in October and connoisseurs tend to prefer the early season birds, especially hens.

Easily identified by the cock bird's gaudy plumage, the pheasant is popular with shooters as a fast flyer and with diners as a flavoursome dish.

HANGING GAME

Game suppliers and butchers will usually have hung, plucked, and drawn game for their customers. But if you shoot or are given pheasants, partridges or grouse 'in the feather' it is usually best to let them hang for a while before preparing them for the table. This helps to tenderise the meat and bring out the flavour.

Gamebirds should be hung in a cool, well ventilated place - and by the neck, not the feet. How long depends on your taste and on the weather conditions, but three or four days will probably be enough for most tastes. Leaving birds to hang for a week or so will produce a more mature flavour. They are ready if the feathers round the tail can be plucked easily.

FOOD HYGIENE

As you will be handling raw and cooked meat, make sure all knives, work surfaces, chopping boards and other utensils are washed thoroughly before and after use.

Check that your fridge is running at the right temperature, about 4°C, and your freezer at minus 18°C or below.

Ensure that cooked and raw game are kept apart - and covered. Thaw frozen game completely before cooking, preferably at room temperature. It should not be refrozen unless cooked. Game dishes should be reheated thoroughly and not more than once. Finally, remember that game may contain a small quantity of lead shot which is best removed before cooking.

Main courses

**Cooking times
and quantities**
Each recipe serves four unless otherwise stated. All cooking times in this book are a guide. They can vary according to the size or age of the gamebird or the type of oven. Allow one gamebird per person, apart from pheasant and mallard which should serve two.

Pheasant with wild mushroom risotto and pine nut salad

When you are buying pheasant, ask for a nice, young bird, preferably a hen, as they don't need to be cooked for as long as an older bird.

Preheat the oven to 200°C. Season the pheasants and seal on all sides in a hot pan with a little vegetable oil. Transfer to the oven and roast for approximately 12 minutes on each leg, then finally for 20 minutes on their backs. Leave somewhere warm to rest.

Risotto Heat a large pan and melt half of the butter, add the shallots and garlic and cook for 3 to 4 minutes until soft. Turn up the heat and add the rice and fry for 2 to 3 minutes.

Add the wine and cook until fully evaporated. Start to add the stock one or two ladles at a time, stirring all the time. When each ladle of stock has evaporated add another. Cook for 15 to 17 minutes until the risotto is al dente.

Meanwhile, sautée the mushrooms in butter and, when they are done, add them to the risotto. Finish with the remaining butter and Parmesan and season.

Make the vinaigrette and toss the rocket and toasted pine nuts in the dressing in a bowl. Spoon the risotto onto each plate, carve a pheasant breast and lay on top. Serve with the rocket and pine nut salad on the side.

Ingredients
Serves four

2 hen pheasants, dressed
2 tbsps vegetable oil

Risotto
300g risotto rice
100g butter
3 shallots, finely chopped
2 cloves of garlic, finely chopped
75ml dry white wine
1 litre hot chicken stock
250g fresh wild mushrooms
75g Parmesan
Salt and ground black pepper
150g rocket
30g pine nuts, toasted

Vinaigrette
30ml red wine vinegar
150ml olive oil
Salt and pepper

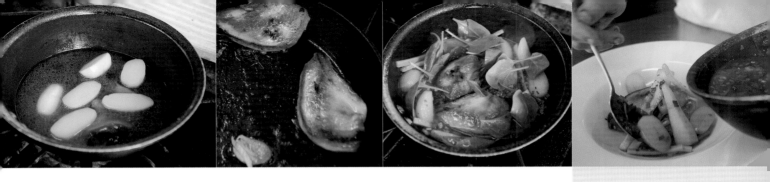

Braised pheasant breast with root vegetables

Parboil new potatoes in water and cut in half lengthways. Also parboil root vegetables of your choice. This can be done well in advance.

Heat the game stock in a separate saucepan, having checked the flavour and seasoned with salt, pepper or sugar as necessary. Add prunes (this gives the stock a richer character).

Place potatoes in the stock, then the root vegetables. Simmer for 10 minutes at most until the vegetables are to your taste.

In a heavy pan fry the breast fillets in a little olive oil, not too quickly, adding a knob of butter once the oil has heated up again. Cook on each side for about three minutes until the pheasant breasts are lightly seared. Do not overheat or else the butter will brown and the outside of the meat will toughen up.

Once the pheasant breasts are ready, place them in the stock with the root vegetables and simmer gently for two or three minutes at most. Finally add baby spinach leaves and chopped spring onions.

Try the sauce one last time and season to taste. Use sugar or honey to sweeten. Serve in soup bowls.

Ingredients
Serves four

Breasts from a brace of pheasants
500ml game stock (recipe, page 17)
Salt and pepper
2 prunes, stoned and chopped
250g new potatoes
250g selection of vegetables (choose from carrots, parsnips, swedes, celery, turnips, onions or sweet potatoes)
1 tbsp olive oil
25g butter
100g baby spinach leaves
2 spring onions, chopped
1 tsp sugar or honey

Roast pheasant stuffed with leeks and roast pears

Start with the stuffing. Peel and finely dice two of the pears and two of the leeks. Sauté in a pan for about two minutes with a knob of butter. Allow to cool.

Once the stuffing has cooled, push your fingers under the breast skin of the pheasant from the leg end and squeeze in the stuffing between the breast meat and skin. This will inject flavour and keep the meat moist.

Preheat the oven to 200°C. Cover the breast with pancetta bacon rashers and roast the pheasant in a well-oiled pan for 30 to 35 minute depending on size. Set aside to rest.

Finely chop the remaining leeks. Sweat down in butter in a pan over a medium heat until tender. Add double cream and cook gently until the cream has reduced slightly.

Cut each remaining pear into six segments lengthways. Melt 25g of butter in a pan until frothing. Add the pears and fry gently for about a minute. Add a sprinkling of sugar, then roast in the oven for 4 to 5 minutes at 200°C until caramelised and tender..

Fondant Potato Peel the potatoes. Cut lengthways into a rectangular or square shape. In a heavy pan melt 10g to 20g of butter on a medium heat until frothing, add potatoes and caramelise top and bottom. For added flavour, you can add a crushed clove of garlic still in its skin.

Pour in chicken stock to half submerge the potatoes, cover whole pan with greaseproof paper and cook in the oven at 200°C until tender. This takes between 10 and 20 minutes depending on the size of the potato.

Sauté the mushrooms in butter and keep warm. Place the ready-made ravioli in boiling water in a saucepan and simmer until al dente. For the sauce, reduce remaining stock (about 250ml) by half and season to taste.

Assembly Carve off the pheasant breast and legs. Top the fondant potato with mushrooms, and decorate with a pheasant leg. Slice the breast in two and place on a pile of leeks. Arrange the ravioli (optional) on top of the breast with a rasher of pancetta and the pears alongside. Add sauce and serve.

Ingredients
Serves two

1 pheasant, dressed
4 pears
4 leeks
100g butter, unsalted
4 slices pancetta bacon
2 tbsps double cream
Salt, pepper and sugar to season
24 trumpet mushrooms (or any other woody wild mushrooms)
500ml game or chicken stock (recipe, page 17)
2 medium potatoes (Maris Piper)
1 clove garlic
2 ready-made mushroom ravioli (optional garnish)

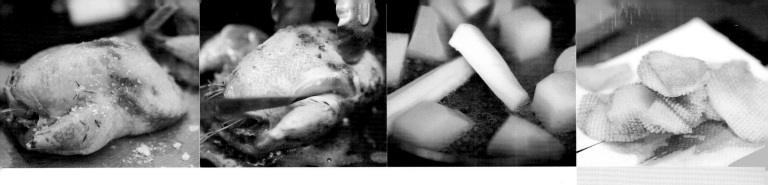

Pot roast partridge with honey roast root vegetables

Everything goes into one pot for this fantastic meal. It's just perfect for all game lovers who don't mind getting their fingers sticky.

Place garlic and thyme in the cavity of each partridge. Heat a large ovenproof frying pan with olive oil and butter. When the oil and butter start to foam add the partridges. Seal birds for two minutes each side until golden brown and remove from the pan.

Wash and peel the vegetables before cutting into 2cm / 1in square chunks. Place vegetables in pan, cover with cold water, add a little salt. Bring to the boil, reduce heat, cook until al dente and strain.

Roast off the vegetables in the frying pan, add thyme and garlic. Deglaze the pan with cider vinegar, stir in the honey and season with salt and pepper. Place the birds on top of the root vegetables and season.

Preheat oven to 200°C and roast for 10 to 15 minutes. Remove from oven, cover with foil and allow to rest for another five minutes or so. By then the juices from the partridge should run clear, not pinkish.

Deglaze the pot roast juices once more with the chicken stock. Drain off the liquid into a small pan and reduce as necessary over moderate heat. Finish the gravy by stirring in four tablespoons of olive oil. Season to taste.

Carve the partridge and serve with the vegetables, gravy and game chips or potato crisps.

Ingredients
Serves four

4 whole dressed partridges
4 cloves garlic, crushed
4 sprigs of thyme
2 tbsps olive oil
2 knobs of butter

Vegetables
2 large carrots
2 large parsnips
1 medium swede
1 sprig of thyme, chopped
1 garlic clove, crushed
4 tbsps cider vinegar
3 tbsps honey
Salt & ground black pepper
150ml chicken or game stock
4 tbsps olive oil

Breast of partridge with onion Tatin and Madeira sauce

Partridge is usually available from the start of the season in September right through to the end of January. Generally it doesn't need hanging but a brace will keep for several days in a cool place.

Remove fillets from each side of the breast with a sharp knife. Heat a little olive oil in a heavy-bottomed frying pan with a crushed clove of garlic and a sprig of thyme. Add the partridge breasts. Once the oil has warmed up again, add a knob of butter.

Seal the partridge breasts until they are lightly browned on one side. Then flip and repeat for the other side. This should take no more than two minutes per side. Just before they are ready add a little sherry vinegar to take the browning off the pan. Season to taste with soy sauce, salt, pepper and (optional) orange zest.

Roll the partridge breasts in the juices, remove from pan and rest on a warm plate for five minutes or so while you finish the vegetables.

Madeira Sauce Add Madeira and white wine to the pan together with garlic, thyme and chicken stock. Bring to the boil and reduce by half. Adjust flavour with salt, pepper, sugar or lemon juice.

Remember that a thin sauce with a good flavour is better than a thick, coating sauce with a bitter, overpowering flavour. So don't over-reduce the sauce or simmer too rapidly.

Place the partridge breasts on a bed of potatoes and spinach with the onion Tatin alongside (see next page for recipes). Serve with the Madeira sauce.

Ingredients
Serves two

Breasts of 2 partridges
(2 halves per serving)
2 tsps olive oil
1 clove garlic
2 sprigs thyme
1 knob butter
2 tsps sherry vinegar
Salt and pepper
Pinch of orange zest
2 tbsps olive oil
1 tsp soy sauce

Madeira sauce
100ml Madeira
1/4 bottle (200 ml) dry white wine
300ml chicken or game stock
Lemon juice and/or sugar to taste
2 cloves garlic, chopped
2 sprigs thyme

Onion Tatin

The Hotel Tatin in the Loire, where the recipe originated in the 19th century, was always popular with local hunters. The story goes that Stéphanie Tatin flirted with one of them and was so distracted she made the first of her famous upside-down tarts by accident.

First step is to make the caramel for the Tatin. Mix white sugar and unsalted butter in a saucepan. Stir and boil until the mixture turns to a golden brown caramel and emulsifies. Spoon into two individual cake or pudding tins.

Poach half onions or banana (large) shallots in seasoned water or stock until tender. This takes about 20 minutes. Remove and season with soy sauce, sherry vinegar, salt and pepper.

Roll out the puff pastry. Place each shallot or halved onion in an individual cake tin on the caramel and place a circle of puff pastry on top. Preheat oven to 200°C and bake for 15 to 20 minutes. As soon as the puff pastry is browned and the caramel is bubbling, loosen round the edges, turn upside down and remove carefully.

Chef's Tip Instead of onions or shallots, the same Tatin recipe can be used for cherry tomatoes or as a pudding with apples, pineapples or pears.

Vegetables Peel and slice new potatoes and sauté raw in olive oil and butter until golden brown. Very thinly sliced potatoes will cook this way without boiling. At most this takes eight minutes or so. Add ribbons of leek and baby spinach leaves, stir fry, season with salt and pepper.

Ingredients
Serves two

Onion or shallot Tatin
50g white sugar
50g butter
1 large onion or
2 banana (large) shallots
Splash of soy sauce
Splash of sherry vinegar
Salt and pepper
100g puff pastry

250g new potatoes
2 tbsps olive oil
50g butter
1/2 leek
100g baby spinach
Salt and pepper

Roast partridge with redcurrant and port sauce

Wrap the partridge in bacon. Heat a heavy bottomed pan with a little of the oil and butter and seal the partridges on the base and both sides - but NOT the breast.

Place breast upwards in an oven pre-heated to 200°C and roast for 10 to 15 minutes. You can take the partridge out of the oven to test by touch. The meat should be slightly springy, not solid. Set aside to rest.

Quarter or halve the sprouts, depending on size, and cook in boiling, salted water until tender. Cook the chestnuts the same way. Fry the finely diced pancetta or bacon in a hot, well-oiled pan until crisp. Reduce heat and add the sprouts and chestnuts to the pan. Season with salt and pepper.

Pommes Anna Slice the potatoes thinly and arrange the slices in an overlapping layer round each of four small rösti pans brushed with vegetable oil and butter. Spread a layer of sliced prunes on top, then add another layer of sliced potatoes. Sprinkle with salt and pepper plus a knob of butter.

Place each pan on a medium heat, caramelise the bottom layer of potato for one to two minutes, then transfer to a hot oven at 200°C for 10 to 15 minutes until golden.

As a garnish, glaze baby shallots in sugar and butter for about 10 minutes over medium heat in a small pan before adding a splash or two of red wine.

In a separate pan, add port and redcurrant jelly to the juices from roasting the partridge. Add stock and bring to the boil, then reduce by half. Finish with a knob of butter, add fresh or frozen redcurrants and warm through. Assemble with the pommes Anna as a base.

Ingredients
Serves four

4 partridges, oven ready
12 slices unsmoked streaky bacon
100g unsalted butter
4 tbsps vegetable oil
500g Brussels sprouts
8 (peeled) chestnuts
50g pancetta or bacon
Salt and pepper

Pommes Anna
4 medium potatoes, peeled
8 pitted prunes, sliced
50g butter
50ml vegatable oil

12 baby shallots
50g butter
2 tsps sugar
50ml red wine

100ml port
200ml game or beef stock
1 tbsp redcurrant jelly
Knob of butter
1 tbsp fresh or frozen redcurrants

Pan-roasted woodcock with rösti potatoes, cabbage and parsnips

In areas where woodcock are plentiful this is a dish for November to January - unless you choose to leave a woodcock or two in the deep freeze to enjoy after the shooting season is over.

Once you have plucked the woodcock singe off the last feathers with a blow torch or over a gas ring and wipe clean with a damp cloth. There is no need to draw woodcock. In fact, you will need the giblets to make the gravy after the woodcock have been roasted.

Heat a lightly oiled, heavy-bottomed frying pan and quickly brown the woodcock on all sides. Add a crushed clove of garlic. Do not use garlic slices as these will burn and turn bitter. Add freshly chopped thyme and baste with more oil and a knob of butter.

Preheat oven to 200°C and roast for five minutes or so in the same pan. Remove from the oven and rest for a further two to three minutes, then joint the woodcock, carve the breast meat from the bone and keep warm.

Remove the giblets from the carcasses and warm lightly in a pan for two minutes with the red wine, then sieve well into another saucepan. Reheat and thicken slightly but do not boil. Add the port and season to taste with lemon or lime juice, salt and pepper.

Heat sauce through and serve with the woodcock placed on top of the rösti and vegetables (recipes, next page) .

Ingredients
Serves two

Two woodcock
(one per serving)
2 tbsps vegetable oil
1 clove garlic
2 sprigs fresh thyme
50g butter
1 small glass red wine
1/2 glass of port
Dash of fresh lemon or lime juice
Salt and pepper

Rösti potatoes, caramelised apples, cabbage and parsnips

Rösti potatoes Grate the potatoes coarsely, then place in a tea towel and squeeze out excess moisture. Season lightly with salt and pepper and a touch of grated nutmeg. Melt butter and fold into the potato.

Use small, non-stick frying pans to create burger-sized potato cakes. Rösti rely on the natural starch in the potato to bind them together as they cook. Fry in a lightly oiled pan, turning once, until golden brown on both sides.

Parsnips, caramelised apples and buttered cabbage Slice the parsnips lengthways and place in a frying pan. Half cover with water and bring to the boil. Add a knob of butter so that the parsnip is fried once the water evaporates. Adjust the heat and season with salt, pepper and freshly chopped thyme. The parsnips should take about five minutes to cook.

The apple segments should be added at this stage and caramelised with sugar and a knob of butter in the same pan.

Place the cabbage in a skillet, half cover with water and bring to the boil. Add a knob of butter, salt and pepper to taste and cover with a lid. Steam gently for three to four minutes.

Ingredients
Serves two

2 large potatoes, peeled
Grated nutmeg
100g unsalted butter
2 small parsnips, peeled
2 sprigs fresh thyme, chopped
1 large Bramley apple, peeled, cored and quartered
1 tsp sugar
1 small cabbage, shredded
Salt and pepper

Hare in red wine with pappardelle

Young hares are best for this classic, northern Italian dish. If you're feeling adventurous, you can make your own pasta, but most supermarkets now stock good quality, fresh varieties.

Heat a large pan with olive oil and fry the hare mince until golden brown. Remove from the pan and drain to remove the excess fat. Then, in the same pan, fry the onion, garlic, leek and carrot.

Return the mince to the pan and add the wine, Passata, chicken stock, bay leaves and thyme. Cook for 25 to 30 minutes over a medium heat until the meat is tender. Remove the bay leaves and thyme, and season with salt and pepper

Pasta Bring a large pot of salted water to the boil and cook the pappardelle for 6 minutes - or according to the instructions on the pack.

Drain the pasta and toss with the hare and red wine sauce. Finish with olive oil and shaved Parmesan.

Ingredients
Serves six to eight

1.5 kg minced hare meat
5 tbsps olive oil
1 onion, finely chopped
4 cloves garlic, finely chopped
1 leek, chopped
1 carrot, chopped
350ml red wine
400ml Passata (creamed tomatoes)
200ml chicken stock
2 bay leaves
Sprig of thyme
Salt and pepper
750g pappardelle pasta
100g Parmesan shavings

Hare pie with sweet potato, carrots and cabbage

This economical but relatively time-consuming recipe uses the hare's legs and leaves the saddle and loin for another dish. The same method can be used for rabbit or shoulder of venison.

Start by making a confit of hare. Place the hare legs in rock salt and black pepper overnight. Next day wipe off the seasoning and place the legs in a thick bottomed saucepan. Cover with vegetable oil and poach on a slow heat for 2 1/2 to 3 hours until the meat starts to fall of the bone.

Remove from the oil and pick the meat off the bone. Mix with the forcemeat from the sausages, pistachios, prunes, parsley and a splash of brandy. Season with salt and pepper. Shape the meat into four 'burgers'.

To make each pie, line a large ladle with overlapping cling film. Lay a slice of Parma ham on top of the cling film, then place a burger in the ladle and fold the ham up round it. Finally wrap the cling film round each filling and transfer to the fridge to 'set'.

For the crust lightly roll the puff pastry and cut into four squares. Brush each pastry square with beaten egg and place the pie filling in the centre. Fold over the corners and shape by hand as in the picture. Dust off any excess flour and brush with beaten egg. Use a sharp knife to score the top into segments from the centre with a sharp knife and bake in a preheated over for about 15 minutes at 200°C.

We used diced sweet potato and carrot as accompaniments but parsnip, turnip, artichoke or swede would do just as well.

Melt a knob of butter in a pan, sweat the diced vegetables, then add half a cup of boiling water and cook for three to four minutes. Finally add chopped cabbage and sage. Cover and steam until the cabbage is tender. This should take no more than eight minutes or so.

Serving suggestion: mashed potato with parsley and gravy from a reduction of game stock (recipe, page 16).

Ingredients
Serves four

4 hare legs
(one per portion)
4 tbsps rock salt
1 tbsp cracked black pepper
600ml vegetable oil
Filling from 4 large pork sausages
40g pistachio nuts, chopped
4 large prunes, chopped
1 tbsp chopped parsley
1 measure brandy
Salt and pepper
8 slices Parma ham
250g puff pastry
1 egg, beaten

Vegetables
2 large carrots, diced
400g diced sweet potato
1/2 small cabbage, chopped
1 tbsp chopped sage

Braised hare with red onion tart Tatin

This rich and hearty dish is perfect for a winter's meal when hare is most readily available.

Joint the hare by removing the front and hind legs and dividing the body into four across the back. Cut the hind legs into two at the knee joint. Save the liver, heart and kidneys.

Marinade all of the meat for 24 hours in the red wine with juniper berries and finely chopped carrots, celery and Spanish onions.

Remove meat, drain off and pat dry. Save the marinade for later. Toss meat in flour. Heat vegetable oil in a large heavy pan and brown hare pieces on both sides. Don't cram your pan. Add more oil as necessary before sealing any more hare pieces.

Preheat oven to 150°C. Place the hare joints in an ovenproof casserole. Add the marinade with its vegetables and top up with chicken stock until the meat is just submerged. Cover the pan, bring to the boil, then place in the oven for two to three hours. Check after two hours and remove once the meat is tender. Season to taste.

Red onion Tatin   Take two red onions, drizzle with vegetable oil and bake for 10 to 15 minutes in a 150°C oven until tender. Cut in half then half slice through again lengthways, leaving them connected at the root. Fan out the onion halves. Then follow the Tatin recipe on page 67.

Just before serving sauté the heart, liver and kidneys with a knob of butter for a minute or so. Allow to rest, then slice. Keep warm and use as a garnish.

Stir fry the spinach in a wok or shallow pan with a knob of butter, salt and pepper. It will need only a few seconds until it has wilted. Set aside for serving.

Ingredients
Serves four

1 hare
1 bottle red wine
1 tsp juniper berries
4 large carrots
2 sticks of celery
2 Spanish onions
2 tbsps flour
3 tbsps vegetable oil
250ml chicken stock

Onion Tatin
2 red onions
200g puff pastry
100g caster sugar
100g butter, unsalted
100g bag baby spinach
Knob of butter, unsalted
Salt and pepper

Rabbit pie with Savoy cabbage and bacon

A traditional combination that enhances the delicate flavour of rabbit.

Remove the rabbit meat in large, boneless pieces. Toss the meat in seasoned flour, heat some olive oil in a pan and start frying the rabbit in small batches until golden brown. Set aside and fry the next batch until all the rabbit is browned.

Add the mushrooms to the pan and fry until golden brown. Deglaze the pan with the white wine and return the rabbit pieces to the pan. Cover with chicken stock and simmer for 45 minutes until the rabbit is cooked and the stock has thickened. Add the chopped tarragon and season with salt and pepper to taste.

Preheat the oven to 200°C. Divide the rabbit mix between four small pie dishes or use one large dish. Cover with puff pastry, brush with beaten egg and bake for 20 to 25 minutes until the pastry turns golden.

For the vegetables, heat a large pan with a little olive oil until hot, then carefully add the bacon and fry for one minute until it starts to brown.

Add the shredded cabbage and mix well. Pour in a cup of cold water and stir fry for three to four minutes until cooked. This way, the cabbage should retain its vibrant, green colour. Season with salt and white pepper and keep warm.

Finally, cook the baby carrots in boiling water for three to four minutes - depending on size - and toss in melted butter and chopped parsley.

Remove the pie from the oven, place on a plate and arrange the vegetables around it.

Ingredients
Serves four

1 large oven-ready rabbit
3 tbsps seasoned flour
4 tbsps olive oil
150g button mushrooms, cut into quarters
200ml dry white wine
500ml chicken stock or water
2 large sprigs of tarragon, chopped
Salt and pepper
250g ready made puff pastry
1 egg, beaten

1 large Savoy cabbage, shredded
4 rashers of thick cut streaky bacon, chopped
1 tbsp olive oil
20 baby carrots
1 cup water
Knob of butter
Chopped parsley

Rabbit with black pudding

This recipe uses the saddle of the rabbit (the loin and fillet) with the meat and skin from the ribs left attached.

Mix black pudding and thyme leaves in a blender until smooth. Run a sausage of the mix along the rabbit loin. Roll up the joint, using the thin flap of rib meat and skin to seal.

Lay a large sheet of cling film on a table and set out a row of bacon rashers, slightly overlapping, with the rabbit on top. Roll the bacon up round the rabbit. Wrap the joint tightly in the cling film and refrigerate for up to 24 hours to set.

Before cooking, remove cling film and seal the rabbit all the way round in a medium hot pan with vegetable oil and a knob of butter. This takes about two minutes. Preheat oven to 200°C and roast for six to eight minutes until the meat is just opaque. Keep warm.

For pommes Anna, see recipe page 69.

While the meat is resting sauté mushrooms with a knob of butter. Set aside.

Cabbage Blanch four outer leaves of cabbage (minus stalks) in boiling salted water for two minutes. Refresh in cold water. Shred remaining leaves and braise in a little butter with a pinch of thyme leaves for 15 minutes on a gentle heat. Allow to cool. Wrap an individual portion in each of the outer leaves and enclose in a tight parcel of knotted cling film. Poach in hot water for about 5 minutes.

Pastry triangles Layer filo pastry sheets with butter in between each layer. Cut into four triangles and bake at 210°C for five minutes or more until golden rown.

Sauce Reduce the red wine and chicken stock by half in a saucepan. Season with salt and pepper. Warm broad beans in the sauce to use as garnish.

Finally, remove the cabbage portions from cling film, carve the rabbit and arrange dish as shown.

Ingredients
Serves four

Saddle of one large rabbit (off bone)
100g black pudding (skin removed)
4 sprigs of thyme
12 slices pancetta bacon
2 tbsps vegetable oil
150g butter
10 cèpes, porcini or shiitake mushrooms
4 medium potatoes (Maris Piper)
8 prunes, pitted
Salt and pepper
1/2 Savoy cabbage
4 sheets filo pastry
200ml chicken stock
1/2 glass red wine
75g broad beans
Salt and pepper

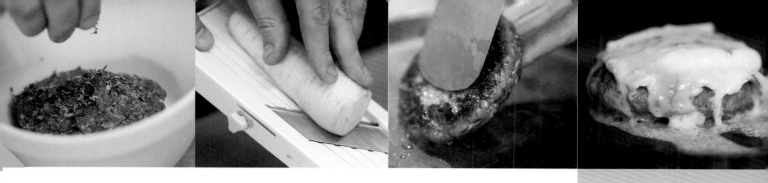

Venison burger with root vegetable crisps and blue cheese

Venison takes over from beef in this recipe to produce a stylish variation of the cheeseburger - and what a difference it makes!

To make the burgers, mix the mince, onion and thyme together, adding salt and pepper to season. If you wish, fry a small piece of the mix and taste it to make sure that the seasoning is just right for you.

Divide the burger mix into four patties and place in the fridge for a couple of hours to firm up.

Finely slice the root vegetables and fry in vegetable oil until crisp. Drain, season with salt and set aside so that they remain crispy.

Heat a frying pan with a little oil and fry the burgers for 4 to 5 minutes on each side - longer if you like them well done.

Place the burgers on a baking tray, add a thick slice of blue cheese and brown under the grill.

Serve the cheeseburgers in a toasted bun with the root vegetable crisps, salad and mustard.

Ingredients
Serves four

600g coarsely minced venison
1 red onion, finely chopped
1 tsp chopped thyme
Sea salt
Ground black pepper
200 ml vegetable oil
1 parsnip
2 carrots
1 celeriac
4 slices blue cheese
4 buns
Seasonal salad
Mustard

Roast saddle of venison with mushrooms and asparagus

This dish features a well-fatted saddle of venison, rolled and tied as in the picture.

Use a heavy-bottomed pan with just enough cooking oil to cover the base. Add a smashed clove of garlic - not slices in case they burn and turn bitter - and seal the venison on all sides. Transfer to a preheated oven at 180°C.

The roasting process depends on the size of the joint but should take only 10 to 15 minutes for rare. Check after five minutes and turn before roasting for another five. To stop the meat sticking to the pan you can roast it on a bed of thick, raw potato slices which are then discarded.

Test the venison by touch once you have taken it out of the oven. A rare joint will still be spongy and becomes firmer as it cooks through. Resting the meat in a warm oven will turn a rare joint to medium rare.

Deglaze the pan juices with the game stock and red wine. Reduce over a medium heat until the gravy coats a wooden spoon. Season with salt and pepper.

Mushrooms (blewitts in the picture) are perfect with venison. The larger ones should be sliced and scored before frying in vegetable oil and butter until golden. Then add leek strips, salt and pepper and heat through.

For the asparagus, lay the trimmed spears flat in a frying pan and half cover with boiling water. Add a knob of butter and cook on a fairly high heat until the water has evaporated and the asparagus has 'roasted' in the butter until it is al dente. Season with salt and pepper and finish with lemon juice.

Serve the carved venison with mushrooms, asparagus and red wine gravy as shown.

Ingredients
Serves six

2 1/2 lb (1.2 kg) saddle of venison
1 clove of garlic
2 tbsps vegetable oil
300ml game stock
1/2 bottle red wine
450g mushrooms of your choice
50g butter
1 large leek, cut into strips
30 asparagus spears
4 cloves garlic
Juice of 1/2 lemon
Salt and pepper

Shoulder of venison with sautéd cauliflower and fondant potato

Bone, roll and tie a shoulder of venison and marinate overnight in half a bottle of red wine with rock salt, 4 cracked juniper berries and mixed peppercorns - white, black and Sichuan (if you can find them).

Remove venison from the marinade and seal on all sides using olive oil in a heavy bottomed pan. Transfer in the same pan to a preheated oven at 200°C and roast for 30 to 40 minutes for a 2 1/2 lb shoulder. Roasting time will depend on the size of the joint. The venison can be placed on a bed of sliced raw potatoes to prevent it sticking to the pan.

Add a small quantity of stock or boiling water to stop the juices burning. Remove from the oven and test the meat by touch. It will be rare if spongy and medium rare as it starts to become firmer. Set the venison aside to rest.

Use the remaining half bottle or red wine and game stock to clear the pan juices. Reduce over a moderate heat until the sauce coats a wooden spoon. Season and keep warm.

Fondant potatoes These can be prepared in advance and reheated. Peel three large potatoes and cut two thick rounds from each (see picture). Place in a pan, just cover with water and add a knob of butter for each slice. Boil until the water evaporates and the butter starts to caramelise the potato slices. Turn in the pan to brown on both sides.

Sautéd cauliflower Split the cauliflower into large florets and blanch with the carrots in boiling water. Drain, then place in a pan with a knob of butter. Season with salt and pepper and fry gently until golden. At the last minute add the carrot strips and freshly chopped parsley.

Cabbage in cream Pour whipping cream into a pan, bring to the boil and fold in finely shredded cabbage with two cracked juniper berries. Simmer until the cabbage is tender but with a slight crunch. Season.

Carve the venison and serve with red wine sauce and vegetables as shown.

Ingredients
Serves six

2 1/2 lb (1.2 kg) shoulder of venison
1 bottle red wine
Good pinch of rock salt
6 cracked juniper berries
1 tsp mixed peppercorns
4 tbsps olive oil
275ml game stock

For the vegetables
3 large baking potatoes
150g butter
1 small cauliflower
2 large carrots, in strips
1 tbsp fresh parsley, chopped
1 small cabbage, shredded
150ml whipping cream
Salt and pepper

HEALTHY EATING

Most people want to eat healthy food. They also want to know how and where it's produced. On both counts British game scores high marks. It can be locally sourced, with full traceability - and it's big on flavour and low in fat.

Venison, for example, is lower in fat and cholesterol than many other red meats as well as being a good source of protein and vitamins. With 35g of protein per 100g, it's the ideal meat for anyone on a high protein, low fat diet.

Research commissioned by **Game-to-Eat** shows that gamebirds are a good source of selenium, an essential trace element that plays an important role in boosting the immune system.

Game is wild, natural and free range - and it's often available from local producers. Coupled with all these benefits, game's distinctive flavour makes it an ideal choice for people who want something delicious and different in their diet.

game-to-eat

Clipsham venison casserole with tarragon juniper dumplings

Sean Hope dedicates this dish to the memory of his father, a real countryman who loved his pheasant and game. The same recipe works well for hare or mixed game.

Preheat the oven to 150°C. Add olive oil to a large frying pan, heat and seal diced venison briskly and in batches. Remove from frying pan, place in a large casserole pan and dust the meat with flour.

Return the frying pan to the heat, add the port and real ale, bring to the boil and then reduce by half. Add to the casserole with the venison.

Wipe out the frying pan with kitchen towel, add a tablespoon of olive oil, toss in prepared vegetables and garlic and fry until golden brown (about 10 minutes).

Place the roasted vegetables in the casserole pan with the venison and add the rest of the ingredients. Cover and place casserole in the oven at 150°C for three hours or until meat is nice and tender. Season to taste and serve.

For the dumplings, mix flour, suet and chopped juniper berries in a bowl. Add English mustard, tarragon and just enough cold water to make a fairly stiff dough. Shape into 12 dumplings.

Thirty minutes before serving, remove the casserole lid, place the dumplings on the surface of the stew and continue to cook until ready.

Ingredients
Serves six

500g diced venison
2-3 tbsps olive oil
1 tbsp plain flour
100ml port or Madeira
300ml real ale
1 large carrot, peeled, roughly chopped
1 turnip, peeled, chopped
1 onion, roughly chopped
1 clove garlic, finely chopped
1 tbsp redcurrant jelly
1 tbsp tomato paste
4 tbsps red wine vinegar
300ml beef stock
1/4 stick cinnamon

Juniper Tarragon Dumplings
175g self-raising flour
75g shredded suet
1 tsp chopped juniper berries
1 tsp English mustard
1 tsp chopped tarragon
Pinch of salt and ground black pepper
100 ml (approx) cold water

Roast haunch of venison

A haunch of venison should be treated the same as a leg of lamb. You can ask your butcher to bone, roll and tie the haunch for you.

Season and seal the haunch on all sides in a large, well-oiled roasting tray. Meanwhile preheat the oven to 200°C. When the venison is sealed, transfer to the oven and roast for about an hour for a medium rare finish, basting occasionally.

Remove the haunch from the oven and leave to rest in a warm place for at least 20 minutes. Meanwhile, place the shallots, juniper berries, peppercorns and red wine vinegar in a saucepan and reduce over a medium heat until the vinegar has evaporated.

Add the red wine and reduce by half, then add the stock and the roasting juices. Reduce the liquid again by half. To finish, stir in 20g of dark chocolate and strain the sauce through a sieve.

Carve the haunch and serve with red wine sauce. For the vegetables select from other recipes in this cook book or serve a combination of your own favourites.

Ingredients

Depending on the size of the haunch, this should serve 8 to 10 people

1 haunch of venison (boned and rolled, about 2kg)
4 tbsp vegetable oil
10 shallots, chopped
10 juniper berries
15 black peppercorns, crushed
75ml red wine vinegar
1/2 bottle red wine
500ml beef stock
20g dark chocolate

Wild duck, curly kale and pear chutney

The chutney in this combination is good all through the winter with terrines, pies and game birds, so this recipe makes plenty for this dish and many more.

Make the chutney in advance. Place the vinegar, sugar, spices, onion and apple in a large pan and bring to the boil. Add all the other ingredients and cook slowly for one to two hours until the chutney has thickened.

Transfer to glass jars when cool, cover with a jam pot cover and lid, and keep in a cool place. If you can wait, leave the chutney for at least a week to let the flavours develop.

Mallard Season and seal the ducks in a hot, well-oiled pan, then roast in the oven for 25 minutes at 200°C for a medium rare finish. Remove from the oven and leave to rest in a warm place. Keep the duck fat for roast potatoes.

Peel and quarter the potatoes, parboil in salted water for five minutes, remove and dry off. Sprinkle with salt and transfer to a pan of the hot duck fat and (if needed) vegetable oil. Baste in the fat and roast at 220°C until golden brown (30 to 40 minutes).

Boil the kale in boiling salted water for five minutes, drain and toss in butter.

Remove the duck breasts and legs, place on the buttered kale and serve with the pear chutney and roast potatoes.

Ingredients
Serves four

2 wild mallards, dressed
2 tbsps vegetable oil
2 heads of curly kale, large stalks removed
Butter
3 large potatoes
Salt and pepper

For the chutney
(makes four 1lb / 500g jars)
250ml cider vinegar
300g sugar
1/2 tsp ground cinnamon
1/2 tsp ground nutmeg
50g fresh ginger, peeled and chopped
1 pinch saffron
1/2 an onion, finely chopped
100g of apple, peeled and grated
500g of pears, peeled and diced
250g of tomatoes, skinned, and chopped
75g sultanas
Juice of 1/2 an orange

Hot smoked goose breast

Unlike a reared bird, wild goose is low in fat and is usually better casseroled or turned into pâté than roasted. If you want to roast wild goose, you usually have to add fat in the form of goose fat or bacon. That isn't necessary in this recipe.

For this recipe (we used a young greylag) take breast meat off the bone and remove skin. Mix the marinade in a bowl, dip the goose breast in the mix and leave in the fridge for several hours, overnight if possible, before you start cooking.

For smoking you can use a small home barbecue with charcoal and oak chips or sawdust. For added flavour try adding some cinnamon stick to the sawdust. Allow the charcoal to burn through, then cool it down with sawdust or oak chips. Don't let the barbecue catch fire again - the goose must be hot smoked, not grilled

Smoke the goose breast on the griddle, covered with the barbecue lid, for 15 minutes or so. Check occasionally that the barbecue is just smoking, adding more sawdust or oak chips as necessary to dampen it down. Set the goose breast aside in tin foil, covered, to rest.

Once cooled, carve the goose breast and season with salt and pepper, plus a squeeze of orange juice.

For the pesto, put blanched parsley, garlic, a few pine nuts and olive oil, in a processor or blenderand blitz for 10 seconds.

Serve the sliced goose with pesto, rocket and parmesan shavings.

Ingredients
Serves four

Breast meat of one goose

For the marinade
One tbsp maple syrup or honey
Pinch of rock salt and cracked black pepper
Two cloves of garlic
Two sprigs of thyme
Cracked Sichuan pepper (if available)

For the pesto
50g blanched parsley
1 clove garlic
1 tbsp pine nuts
100ml olive oil

Squeeze of orange juice
50g rocket
100g Parmesan shavings
Salt and pepper

Potted goose leg

This is a traditional recipe using a method popular for potted shrimps or beef.

Start with two goose legs saved from the smoked goose recipe (page 99). Roll each goose leg in the dry marinade and leave for 24 hours. This draws the moisture from the meat and helps to break it down while cooking.

Once the goose legs are ready, brush off the marinade and gently poach in vegetable oil for about one and a half hours. The trick is to leave the goose legs slowly ticking over until the meat is tender and just about ready to drop off the bone. Drain and allow to cool.

Break up the meat - don't smash it - into a bowl and add chopped spring onions, shallots and a teaspoon of honey. Season to taste with salt and pepper, plus a splash of orange and lemon juice. If the meat looks dry, add a teaspoon of olive oil.

Melt the butter, seasoned with a pinch of mace and a small pinch of cayenne pepper. Add a tablespoonful each of roasted pine nuts and roasted, broken hazelnuts.

Place goose mix in a bowl, press down lightly and pour the nuts and butter slowly over the mix. Place the bowl in a fridge to set. Serve with crusty bread.

Ingredients
Serves four as a starter or two as a main course

2 goose legs
500 ml vegetable oil
2 spring onions
1 shallot
1 tsp honey
Juice of 1/2 lemon
Splash of fresh orange juice
1tsp olive oil
Salt and pepper
125g butter
Pinch of mace
Pinch of cayenne pepper
1 tbsp roasted pine nuts
1 tbsp broken hazelnuts

For the marinade
4 juniper berries, crushed
2 sprigs of thyme, chopped
1 clove garlic, minced
1 bay leaf, chopped
Pinch of Chinese five-spice
Pinch of sugar
Cracked black pepper
and rock salt
(pinch of each)

Mallard with creamed chicory and fondant potato

The richness of duck's breast combines with the subtle flavours of creamed chicory to provide a hearty winter's meal.

Take duck breasts off the bone. Heat vegetable oil in a heavy-bottomed pan and seal the breasts, skin side down, for up to three minutes over a medium heat. Remove from the heat and take off the skin.

Return duck to the heated pan, add a knob of butter and reseal on both sides. This should take two to three minutes for each side. Remove from the heat and set aside to rest.

For the creamed chicory, place individual chicory leaves in a heated wok with a splash of olive oil. Add a pinch each of salt, pepper and sugar to help the chicory caramelise.

Once the leaves are tender and turning brown, add whipping or double cream. Bring to the boil, slightly reduce and check seasoning again.

Serve with carved duck breast on top of the chicory with fondant potato (recipe, page 89) and Madeira sauce (recipe, page 65).

Ingredients
Serves two

1 mallard, plucked and drawn
2 tbsps vegetable oil
25g butter
2 bulbs of chicory (endive)
2 tsps olive oil
Pinch of salt, pepper and sugar
50ml whipping or double cream

Mallard with blood orange sauce

For all who enjoy the duck-and-orange combination, this is a true classic!

Make the risotto first. Finely chop the shallots and sauté with a knob of butter until soft but not coloured. Add risotto rice and cook gently for two minutes.

Add red wine and cook over a medium heat, stirring ontinuously, until absorbed. This takes about two minutes. Next, add chicken stock a ladle at a time, allowing each to be absorbed before adding another.

After using about 200ml of the stock check the rice to see if it is al dente. Add more stock as necessary. Remove from heat, stir in Parmesan and remaining butter. Season to taste.

Pour rice onto a deep tray to a depth of about 3 cm / 1 in and allow to cool. Using a circular pastry cutter, separate four rounds of risotto rice about 7cm in diameter and place on a tray. Before serving reheat in the oven at 180°C for 5 minutes.

For the duck, heat vegetable oil in a large heavy-bottomed pan. Seal each bird on all sides until golden. Preheat oven to 200°C and roast for 20 minutes or so. Allow to rest for 5 to 10 minutes. Remove breasts and legs. Keep warm.

Zest two of the blood oranges, peel and carve into segments. Juice the remaining two. Reduce juice by half over a medium heat, add remaining (about 500ml) chicken stock and reduce again by at least half. Season with salt and pepper.

Cook halved baby turnips in boiling salted water until tender. Sauté wild mushrooms in a little vegetable oil with the cooked turnips. Season with salt and pepper.

To finish, add orange segments and zest to the sauce and warm through.

Ingredients
Serves four

2 mallards (plucked and drawn)
300g risotto rice
100g butter, unsalted
2 banana shallots
(or 4 small shallots)
4 glasses red wine
1 litre chicken stock
100g freshly grated Parmesan

2 tbsps vegetable oil
4 blood oranges
12 baby turnips
200g wild mushrooms, preferably chanterelles
Salt and pepper

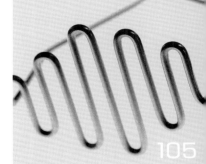

105

Roast grouse with red wine sauce and bread sauce fritters

Grouse are easy to overcook, and most people prefer them slightly pink. Young grouse particularly need to be treated with respect. You could just about pan-roast them from start to finish without using the oven.

Cover grouse breasts with smoked bacon, place in a medium hot, heavy-bottomed frying pan with vegetable oil and a knob of butter. Crush a couple of garlic cloves (leave the skin on) and place them in the pan together with the thyme. Do not chop the garlic as it is more likely to burn and turn bitter.

Over a medium heat, seal the grouse on one side, then the other, then the breast. Finally cook it with the back down. The entire process should take about ten minutes - two minutes each for the leg sides, two minutes on each side of the breast, and two minutes for the back.

Set aside in a warm place to allow the grouse to rest for five minutes or so. Resting allows the meat and juices to stabilise and tenderise. It should then be ready to serve. If not, finish in the oven at 180°C for four to five minutes.

For the red wine sauce, see recipe on page 21. The recipe for bread sauce fritters is on the next page.

Ingredients
Serves two

Brace of young grouse
4 rashers smoked bacon
2 tbsps vegetable oil
50g butter
2 garlic cloves
2 sprigs thyme

Red wine sauce
1 glass of red wine (150 ml)
1/2 glass port
200 ml chicken stock

Bread sauce fritters, buttered cabbage

To make the fritters you will need to have cooked mashed potato and vegetables from an earlier meal. This makes it an ideal dish for leftovers.

Infuse the milk with two cloves, a quarter of star anise, a pinch of cinnamon and half a clove of garlic. Take four thick slices of white bread and chop into cubes.

Warm the milk through, then sieve to remove the cloves, garlic etc. Add bread cubes. Season with salt and pepper and cook on low heat for five minutes, stirring regularly. Set aside.

Combine the bread sauce with two tablespoons each of mashed potato and leftover vegetables, as available. We used diced carrots, leeks and spring onions. Check the seasoning.

Heat a knob of butter or a splash of vegetable oil in a small non-stick pan, and spoon in a serving of the fritter mixture. Brown on one side and turn to brown on the other. Set each aside and keep warm.

Buttered Cabbage Shred Savoy cabbage and blanch for two minutes in salted boiling water, then strain. Add a knob of butter, and salt and pepper to taste. Finish with a dash of lemon juice.

Before serving add the blackberries to the red wine sauce (previous page) and warm through. Serve the grouse whole with the cabbage and fritters alongside.

Ingredients
Serves two

For the bread sauce fritters
2 tbsps mashed potato
250ml milk
2 cloves
1/2 star anise
1/2 clove garlic
Pinch of cinnamon
1/2 clove garlic
4 thick slices white bread
Salt and pepper
2 tbsps leftover vegetables
(e.g. cooked carrots, leeks, cabbage or parsnips)

100g Savoy cabbage
Juice of 1/2 lemon
12 blackberries (optional)

A huge variety of seasonal and imported fruits and vegetables can now be teamed up with the best of British game.

More and more restaurants are adding game to their menus - and home chefs are following the trend

Desserts

Apple and Stilton tart

People who have only ever encountered Stilton on a cheese board may think this is an unusual combination. They should try it!

First, the grape chutney. Put all ingredients in a pan and bring to the boil. Lower heat and simmer. Stir regularly until the chutney reaches jam consistency. Allow to cool, then season with lemon juice and/or sugar.

Preheat the oven to 180°C. Roll out puff pastry until about 1/8 in (3mm) thick. Cut into four 4in x 2in (10cm x 5cm) rectangles and place on a baking tray. Season with salt and pepper. To allow the puff pastry to rise evenly, place a wire cooling rack on top of the pastry when cooking. Bake for 15 to 20 minutes and set aside to cool.

Peel, quarter and core the apples. Cut each quarter into half again. Roll in sugar and heat gently in a pan with knob of butter until caramelised.

Spread a tablespoon of grape chutney onto each pastry base, then arrange apple quarters on top with layers of Stilton in between and on top of the apple. Return to the oven for 5 to 10 minutes until the Stilton has melted.

For a savoury dressing (optional) mix a vinaigrette of olive oil and aged balsamic vinegar and drizzle round the plate as shown. Any extra chutney can be refrigerated for later use.

Ingredients
Makes four individual tarts

250g puff pastry
Salt and pepper
2 large eating apples
200g Stilton
4 tbsps grape chutney

Grape chutney
1kg white grapes
100ml white wine vinegar
1 cinnamon stick
50g sugar
Splash of lemon juice

Dressing (optional)
2 tbsps olive oil
1 tbsp balsamic vinegar

Blackberry compote

This eye-catching dessert is so easy to make and takes advantage of all the wild brambles that usually produce a good crop of blackberries.

Place blackberries in a pan with water, sugar, vanilla seeds and pod. Add the orange and lemon zest. Cook on a low heat for 20 minutes. Do not boil. Place in a container and leave to cool. Add lemon juice to taste.

Place crème fraîche in a large bowl. Cut open the vanilla pod lengthways and scrape out the seeds. Add seeds to the crème fraîche. Sieve in icing sugar to taste and whisk until thoroughly mixed.

Place crème fraîche in the bottom of a glass, then add a layer of blackberries, then another layer of crème fraîche and so on. Serve with shortbread biscuits.

Shortbread biscuits Place all ingredients in a bowl and mix using a paddle attachment until the mixture forms small walnut-sized pieces. Knead by hand until all the mixture comes together.

Roll out on a lightly floured surface until the shortbread is about 1cm or just less than 1/2 inch thick. Cut into 12cm / 5 inch long strips and leave to rest in the fridge for 20 minutes.

Cook at 160°C for 20 minutes or until lightly browned. Remove from oven and sprinkle with caster sugar.

Ingredients
Serves four

400g blackberries
(fresh or frozen)
Water to cover
Caster sugar to taste
Vanilla pod, scraped
Zest of one lemon
Zest of one orange
Squeeze of lemon juice
400ml crème fraîche

Shortbread biscuits
250g plain flour
150g unsalted butter
75g caster sugar

119

Crème brûlée with poached rhubarb

Crème brûlée can so easily split or scramble, so extra care is needed with this recipe.

Place egg yolks in a bowl and mix together with a whisk. Place cream, milk, sugar and vanilla pod - the vanilla seeds are scraped into the mix - in a pan and bring to the boil. Pour onto the egg yolks, stirring continuously.

Return to the pan, whisking constantly and cook over a low heat until the vanilla pod no longer sinks and the mixture coats the back of a spoon. Do not allow to boil.

Pass the mixture through a sieve, pour into oven proof moulds and cook in the oven for 20 to 30 minutes at 120°C until just set. Allow to cool and refrigerate.

Finally, scatter the tops with a thin layer of caster sugar and caramelise under a hot grill or with a blow torch.

Poached Rhubarb Cut rhubarb into equal strips as shown. Add grenadine and sugar to 600ml (1 pint) of water in a pan, stir and bring to the boil.

Remove the pan of syrup from the heat and immediately put in the rhubarb. Cover the pan with a lid or cling film. Leave rhubarb to poach as the syrup cools.

Serving suggestion Serve the rhubarb in a similar mould to the crème brûlée with a scoop of your favourite sorbet alongside.

Ingredients
Serves four

4 egg yolks
300ml double cream
100ml milk
75g caster sugar
1 vanilla pod (split and scraped)
2 tsps sugar for caramelising

Poached Rhubarb
350g rhubarb
2 tbsps grenadine syrup
250g sugar

Apple pie

Not everyone will go to the trouble of making individual apple pies, so feel free to use this recipe to make one large pie.

Sift flour into a food processor and add slices of butter. Process until the mixture resembles fine breadcrumbs. Combine icing sugar and egg yolks in a bowl and add to the flour and butter. Continue mixing until the pastry starts to come together. Remove and knead by hand. Wrap pastry in cling film and refrigerate for at least two hours or overnight.

Grease six individual pie tins. Roll out pastry to desired thickness. Cut out 12 circles of pastry large enough to leave a lip overhanging the tin. Line each of the tins with a pastry circle, pushing the pastry all the way into the edges of the tin. The six remaining circles will be used as pie tops. Refrigerate pastry for about an hour.

Cover the bases with greaseproof paper covered with baking beans and blind bake for 10 to 15 minutes at 180°C. Remove beans and cook for a further 5 minutes until the pastry is golden brown.

Peel, quarter and core six apples and halve each quarter again. Add a little oil and a couple of knobs of butter to a large frying pan, cook for 2 to 3 minutes. Sprinkle apples with a little caster sugar and cook for a further minute. Layer the apples evenly into the tartlets.

Brush the lip of the pastry cases with egg yolk or water and cover each pie with one of the pastry tops, pressing the top down to seal the pie. Brush the top with egg yolk and sprinkle with caster sugar.

Cook for 15 to 20 minutes at 180°C until golden brown. Leave to cool for 10 to 15 minutes. Trim the overhanging edges and remove from tin.

Serve with crème fraîche or custard (recipe, page 131).

Ingredients
Serves six

Six medium eating apples
375g plain flour
225g unsalted butter
50g unsalted butter
1 tbsp caster sugar
150g sieved icing sugar
Two or three egg yolks

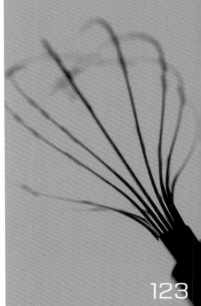

Raspberry cocktail

This great dessert in a cocktail glass tastes and looks a million dollars.

Place crème fraîche in a large bowl. Cut open the vanilla pod lengthways, scrape out the seeds and add them to the crème fraîche. Sieve in icing sugar to taste and whisk until thoroughly mixed.

For serving you will need four cocktail glasses. Place some crème fraîche in the bottom of each glass, then add a layer of raspberries, then another layer of crème fraîche and so on.

Serve with shortbread biscuits (recipe, page 119).

Serve with shortbread biscuits (recipe, page 119).

Ingredients
Serves four

400g fresh raspberries
400ml crème fraîche
1 vanilla pod
Icing sugar to taste

Shortbread biscuits
250g plain flour
150g unsalted butter
75g caster sugar

Chocolate pavé

This is quite a time-consuming dessert but for chocoholics it's well worth the trouble

Sponge Preheat oven to 180°C. Sieve icing sugar and cocoa powder together. Whisk eggs briskly until pale. Fold in icing sugar and cocoa powder. Spread thinly onto a small, greaseproof lined tray and bake for 10 minutes. When cooked the sponge should spring back when pressed. Leave to cool and then remove.

White mousse Place white chocolate in a bowl over hot water to melt. Soften one leaf of gelatine in a small pan with 50ml of water. When gelatine is soft place on a low heat to melt. Whisk melted gelatine into melted chocolate and leave to cool. When the mix is cold, whip cream until soft peaks are formed and fold slowly into the chocolate.

Dark mousse Melt dark chocolate in a bowl over hot water. Place egg yolks in mixing bowl and use an electric whisk at high speed until they start to increase in volume. Reduce the speed, add coffee slowly, then turn the speed up again and mix until the eggs have risen to full volume. Gently stir the dark chocolate and slowly add half of the egg mixture and whisk in by hand. Lightly whip the cream, add half of it to the chocolate and mix. Finally add the remaining egg mixture and fold into the chocolate, then fold in the rest of the whipped cream.

To assemble, use a lined loaf tin. Cut part of the sponge to form a base and place in tin. Pipe white chocolate mousse onto the sponge, then pipe on dark chocolate, layering with additional sponge as desired. Chill in fridge until required.

Chocolate sauce Melt chocolate over hot water. Mix milk, cream and sugar in a pan and heat until sugar has dissolved. Pour slowly over chocolate and whisk. Whisk in unsalted butter until melted.

Remove pavé from tin, cut into portions and serve with the warm chocolate sauce.

Ingredients
Serves six

Sponge
3 eggs
75g icing sugar
50g cocoa powder

White mousse
200g white chocolate
1 leaf of gelatine
50ml water
200ml whipping cream

Dark mousse
200g dark chocolate (70 % cocoa)
4 egg yolks
100ml strong black coffee
200ml whipping cream

Chocolate Sauce
175g dark chocolate (70 % cocoa)
150ml milk
25ml double cream
25g caster sugar
25g unsalted butter

127

Bramley apple and blackberry crumble with cinnamon clotted cream

Here's a popular pudding that features on many country restaurant menus during the shooting season.

Peel, core and roughly chop the apples, melt the butter in a pan, add the apple and cook on high heat until soft. Add the apple juice and sugar, simmer for 3 to 4 minutes and remove from the heat. Leave to cool before adding the blackberries.

To make the crumble, place all the ingredients in a large bowl and rub through your fingers until the mixture resembles breadcrumbs.

Place the apple and blackberry mix in four small, round baking dishes, divide the crumble between them and bake for approx 15 to 20 minutes at 180°C.

For an extra crispy topping, cook the crumble top separately until it's golden brown, then put on top of the apples and blackberries in the individual dishes and bake again.

Before serving mix the clotted cream with caster sugar and a pinch or two of cinnamon and serve on top of the crumble.

Ingredients
Serves four

4 Bramley apples
100g fresh blackberries
30g unsalted butter
100ml apple juice
50g caster sugar

For the crumble
75g unsalted butter, diced
130g light brown sugar
200g plain flour

For the cream
250g clotted cream
1/2 tsp caster sugar
Cinnamon

Plum and almond tart
with English custard

**Once you have made the almond mix, this pudding
can be put together very quickly.**

Beat butter and sugar until pale, add the egg and half of the ground almonds
and mix well. Then add the rest of the almonds and refrigerate until needed.

Roll out the puff pastry until about 3mm / 1/8in thick and cut into rounds using a
saucer or small plate. Spread a little of the almond mix on each tart base,
leaving a small gap around the edges.

Cut the plums in half and remove the stones, slice thinly and arrange the slices
on the pastry discs. Put the tarts back in the fridge while you make the custard.

Custard Split the vanilla pod and scrape the seeds into the milk and cream,
then simmer for 2 to 3 minutes and leave to infuse. Meanwhile, whisk the eggs
and sugar until pale and pour the milk and cream over the eggs and sugar and
return to the pan.

Stir the custard on a low heat until it starts to thicken. When it's ready, pick up
some custard on the back of a wooden spoon and run your finger through it -
the line your finger has left on the spoon should remain clear. Remove custard
from the stove. To prevent overcooking the custard can be passed through a
sieve at this stage into a clean pan or bowl.

Next, heat the oven to 200°C, place tarts on a lined baking tray, sprinkle with
icing sugar and bake for about 20 minutes.

To serve, place each tart on a plate, dust with icing sugar and spoon the custard
around it. This pudding is great with a scoop of vanilla ice cream or a sorbet as
shown.

Ingredients
Serves four

200g ready made puff
pastry
75g soft butter
75g caster sugar
1 egg
75g ground almonds
4 ripe plums
2 tsps icing sugar
4 scoops vanilla ice cream

Custard
4 egg yolks
100ml full fat milk
200ml double cream
1 vanilla pod
75g caster sugar

Vanilla rice pudding with Agen prunes and brandy

A good rice pudding is the ultimate comfort food, whether it's served hot with prunes or winter fruit purées or cold in the summer with strawberries and raspberries.

Place the prunes in a bowl, cover with brandy and, if possible, leave to infuse for a couple of days. If you don't like prunes or brandy, rum and raisins are a good alternative.

Place the rice, milk, sugar, nutmeg and vanilla seeds in a pan and simmer gently for 30 mins until tender. Keep an eye on it at this stage, as it can easily stick to the bottom of the pan. Remove from the heat, add the double cream and keep warm until needed.

To serve, pour the hot rice pudding mix into individual ramekins and place the soaked prunes or raisins on top.

Ingredients
Serves four

100g pudding rice
120ml full fat milk
100g caster sugar
Grated nutmeg
400ml double cream
1 vanilla pod, halved, with the seeds scraped out
200g Agen prunes
150ml brandy

133

Sticky toffee pudding and rock salt caramel

First made famous in Brittany, the flavour combination of salt and caramel gives this classic pudding a subtle twist.

Preheat the oven to 180°C. Place the chopped dates, water and bicarbonate of soda in a small pan and simmer for 5 to 6 minutes, then leave to cool.

Meanwhile, cream the butter and sugar together until pale. Add the egg, sifted flour and baking powder and finally, the cooled date mixture.

Half fill four buttered individual pudding moulds or one large one. Bake for 20 to 25 minutes if using individual dishes, or 40 minutes for a larger dish.

Caramel Place all the ingredients except the salt in a pan and simmer until the mixture turns a rich caramel colour. Then add the rock salt, preferably Maldon or Fleur de Sel.

Loosen the puddings and tip out into serving dishes. Pour the rock salt caramel over the top and serve with a scoop of ready-made vanilla ice cream.

Ingredients
Serves four

130g dates, chopped
200ml water
1/2 tsp bicarbonate of soda
50g soft, unsalted butter
150g dark brown sugar
1 egg
200g self-raising flour
1 tsp baking powder
4 scoops vanilla ice cream

Caramel
250g caster sugar
200ml double cream
200g unsalted butter
1 tbsp rock salt

Oven baked apple with cinnamon clotted cream

Autumn is the ideal time of year to indulge in delicious local apples - adding apple juice will give them a richer flavour.

Mix all stuffing ingredients together in a small saucepan over medium heat for two minutes.

Preheat oven to 190°C. Stand the apples, cored and scored around the middle, in an ovenproof dish. Press a knob of butter and a teaspoon of demerara sugar into each apple together with the stuffing.

Pour apple juice into the ovenproof dish, adding lemon grass and cinnamon to finish. Bake apples for 15 minutes or until slightly soft but not disintegrated.

Remove and allow baked apples to cool. Strain off the juices into a small pan and, over a medium heat, reduce liquid to a syrup.

Puff pastry base   Roll out the puff pastry to a thickness of 3mm / 1/8in. Cut out eight circles of pastry about 10 cm / 4in in diameter. Brush four circles with beaten egg to use as the base of each serving. Use a 5cm / 2in cutter to cut out the centre of the remaining four pastry circles. Place each outer ring of pastry onto one of the bases. The rings will hold the apple in place.

Place the pastry cases on a baking tray lined with greaseproof paper and set one baked apple into each. Bake at 200°C for about 12 minutes until pastry has risen.

Remove from oven and place on a serving dish. Pour over the reduced syrup and finish with a dollop of clotted cream sprinkled with a mixture of caster sugar and cinnamon.

Ingredients
Serves four

Stuffing
2 tbsps suet
4 tbsps toasted almonds
1 tsp allspice
1 tbsp mixed peel
1 tsp marmalade
4 tbsps sultanas
2 tbsps Amaretto liqueur

4 Cox's apples
250ml apple juice
4 tsps demerara sugar
1/2 stick cinnamon
4 knobs of butter
1 stick of lemon grass
(bruised with back of knife)
400g puff pastry
1 egg, beaten

4 tbsps clotted cream
1 tbsp caster sugar
Pinch of cinnamon

Pear tart Tatin with five spice custard

This is a French classic with a touch of Asian influence in the five spice custard. As with many classic dishes, the idea is brilliantly simple - an upside down tart with caramelised fruit. It's extremely versatile and can easily take on a savoury role.

Mix white sugar and unsalted butter in a saucepan. Stir and boil until the mixture turns to a golden brown caramel and emulsifies. Spoon into individual tins or rösti pans and leave to set.

Peel the pears, slice and fan them out on the caramel base. Remember to put the nicest looking slices on the base, which ends up on top. Apples are a good alternative.

Roll out puff pastry to a thickness of about 1/8in / 3mm and cut out a circle slightly larger than the tart case. Tuck inside the case and round the edge of the pears. This creates a 'nest' of pastry.

Bake in a hot oven at about 200°C until the pastry is golden brown and crispy. Remove, allow to cool and carefully turn out upside down onto a plate.

For the custard, follow the recipe on page 131. The only difference is that you infuse the milk with five spice, not vanilla.

Ingredients
Serves four

4 pears (Comice)
100g caster sugar
100g unsalted butter
300g puff pastry

Custard
100ml full fat milk
200ml double cream
4 egg yolks
75g caster sugar
1 tsp five spice

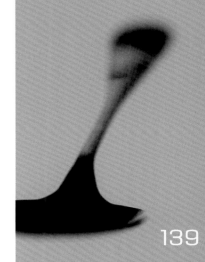

Christmas pudding ice cream with warm mulled wine fruits

Most people eat Christmas pudding only once or twice a year. Here's a variation on that theme.

Place prunes, dried apricots, figs, dates and raisins in a pan and add red wine, cinnamon and twists of orange zest. Bring to the boil, then simmer until the fruit is starting to soften. Only then add fresh pears.

Remove from heat once the pears have turned colour and softened slightly. Set aside.

For the ice cream, all you need is a tub of your favourite ready-made vanilla and a small Christmas pud.

Cook the pud and let it cool. Allow the ice cream to thaw slightly. Crumble the pudding, adding the brandy, and stir into the ice cream. Freeze.

Serve as shown with a twist of orange zest on top of the ice cream.

Ingredients
Serves four

Marinated fruits
100g prunes (pitted)
100g dried apricots
100g dried figs
50g dried dates (pitted)
50g raisins
750ml bottle red wine
Twists of zest from one orange
2 pears, Williams or Comice, peeled, cored and sliced
1 stick cinnamon bark
2 pears, cored and sliced

Ice cream
500ml tub of vanilla Ice cream
1 small Christmas pudding
25ml brandy

Strawberry treacle tart with strawberry ripple ice cream

Local strawberries eaten in the autumn always seem to recall the heady days of summer. This dessert looks good and tastes even better.

Roll out the pastry and fold into an 8in / 20cm flan case. Preheat oven to 180°C. Cover the base with greaseproof paper covered with baking beans to stop it lifting. Blind bake for 10 minutes or so until the pastry starts to brown. Remove from oven.

Scatter the sliced strawberries onto the pastry case. Mix all the other tart ingredients together in a large bowl, then spoon the mixture into the pastry case covering the strawberries.

Place on a warmed baking sheet and bake in oven at 180°C for 20 minutes. Remove and allow to cool slightly before serving with strawberry ripple ice cream.

Strawberry ripple ice cream Take a tub of your favourite vanilla ice cream from the freezer, thaw slightly and soften with a spoon.

Place icing sugar, strawberries and a squeeze of lemon in a blender and purée. Remove and sieve out the seeds. Ripple the coulis through the softened vanilla ice cream and return to freezer to chill for ten minutes or so. Reserve some of the coulis to serve with the tart and ice cream as shown.

Ingredients
Serves 8

Tart
300g shortcrust pastry
300g strawberries, thinly sliced
200g golden syrup
2 tbsps black treacle
275g breadcrumbs from leftover bread
Zest and juice of 2 unwaxed lemons
2 eggs

Ice cream
300 ml ready made ice cream
100g icing sugar
100g strawberries
Squeeze of lemon

Baked chocolate fondant with ginger ice cream and hot chocolate sauce

They say chocolate is the way to a woman's heart - and that probably goes for quite a few men, too. This pud is no exception.

For the chocolate sauce boil double cream with a sprinkling of sugar. Take dark chocolate – 70% cocoa is a must - break or cut it into chunks and melt in the boiled cream away from the heat. Stir until smooth.

Making the ice cream is just as easy. Allow your favourite vanilla ice to thaw slightly. Grate stem ginger into it and add a little syrup from the ginger jar. Mix and return to freezer.

For the fondant, melt dark chocolate and butter in a bowl over boiling water. Whisk together eggs and sugar. Fold in flour, then dark chocolate.

Take a pudding bowl or ramekin, butter the inside and dust with sugar. Spoon in the mix. Bake in the oven at 180°C for six to eight minutes. Test with a knife to ensure the centre is still soft and gooey.

Turn out onto a serving plate, pour on chocolate sauce and top with a scoop of ginger ice cream as shown.

Ingredients
Serves four

Chocolate sauce
75g dark chocolate
(70% cocoa solid)
125ml double cream
25g caster sugar

300ml vanilla ice cream
3 pieces preserved stem ginger
1 tbsp ginger syrup

Fondant
100g dark chocolate
(70% cocoa solid)
100g unsalted butter
3 eggs
100g caster sugar
100g plain flour

Passion fruit tart with honeyed mascarpone cream

This recipe features a delicious contrast between the tartness of passion fruit and the richness of mascarpone.

Roll out the pastry, cut and fold into four individual fluted tart cases . Preheat oven to 180°C. Cover each base with greaseproof paper covered with baking beans to stop it lifting.

Blind bake for 10 to 15 minutes until the pastry starts to turn golden brown. Remove from oven, take out baking beans and greaseproof and return to the oven briefly to dry out the base.

For the custard filling, take a pan and add lemon juice and half the sugar to the passion fruit pulp. Bring to the boil and set aside.

Whisk egg yolks and remaining sugar in a bowl until creamed. Strain in the cooled passion fruit and lemon mix. Pour in double cream and stir until mix is incorporated.

Pour mix into each pastry case, turn down the oven to 150°C and bake for 15 to 20 minutes until the mix is set. Check by wobbling the pastry case to ensure the mix does not overcook. It should still wobble slightly without solidifying.

Allow to cool before dusting with a little caster sugar and caramelising the top with a blow torch or under the grill.

Mix heather honey into mascarpone and shape with two dessertspoons before serving alongside.

Ingredients
Serves four

300g shortcrust pastry
Juice of 1 lemon
120g caster sugar
Pulp of 4 passion fruit
4 egg yolks
100ml double cream
150g mascarpone
2 tsps heather honey

Quince and goat's cheese tart

The quince works well with the subtle flavour of goat's cheese and makes for a great autumn dessert.

You will need a 20cm flan ring, lined with shortcrust pastry blind baked in advance (page 143).

Peel and quarter quinces and remove the core. Place in a saucepan with cinnamon, star anise, water, sugar and lemon juice. Simmer gently for one hour until the quinces are soft and red. Drain and reserve the juices. Allow to cool.

Break goat's cheeses into pieces and place in a mixing bowl (mascarpone can be used as an alternative). Add crème fraîche and blend to make a smooth paste. Lightly whip the whipping cream, add to the bowl with sugar and lime juice and mix thoroughly.

Soak leaves of gelatine in cold water for five minutes. Remove and place in a small pan with two tbsps of the mixture. Stir over a low heat until the gelatine has dissolved.

Add contents of the pan to the rest of the mixture. Stir in vanilla essence. Arrange the cooked quinces on the base of the pastry case and pour the mixture on top. Use a palette knife or the back of a spoon to smooth over.

Refrigerate the tart for one hour and allow to set before removing from the flan ring. Over a medium heat, reduce the cooking juices from the quinces to a syrup and drizzle over each portion. Dust with icing sugar before serving.

Ingredients
Serves four

300g shortcrust pastry
4 ripe quinces
1 stick of cinnamon
1 star anise
600ml water
450g sugar
Juice of 1 lemon

2 soft-sided 100g goat's cheeses (mild)
2 tbsps crème fraîche
Juice of one large lime
2 heaped tbsps of caster sugar
2 drops vanilla essence
300ml whipping cream
2 leaves of gelatine
Icing sugar

Poached pineapple with Sichuan pepper

Pineapple makes a really refreshing dessert and the Sichuan pepper gives it a spicy, oriental flavour that goes perfectly with a sorbet.

Cut the top and bottom off the pineapple. Keeping the pineapple upright, remove the skin and cut into quarters lengthways. Then cut each quarter into thirds.

Add the Sichuan pepper and 100g of the sugar to the water in a pan. Place on the stove, stir and bring to the boil.

Immediately remove pan from the heat, place pineapple into the hot syrup and cover with the lid slightly off to allow steam to escape.

Once the pineapple has cooled down completely, drain well and roll in remaining sugar. Place pineapple in a hot, non-stick frying pan, turning until caramelised.

Serve with a portion of mango or passion fruit sorbet, or alternatively with vanilla ice cream. These days you can buy any of them without going to the trouble of making your own.

Ingredients
Serves four

1 pineapple
1 tbsp Sichuan pepper
150g sugar
750 ml water for syrup
300 ml ready made ice cream or sorbet

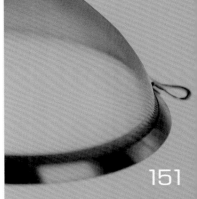

Sales of game

For many years sales of game such as pheasant, partridge and grouse have been regulated by Game Acts introduced long before the invention of the deep freeze. These restrict sales of game to the relevant season plus a further 10 days once the season is over. Game may be sold only by licensed game dealers.

Sales of venison are not seasonally restricted, while wild duck may be sold at any time from September through February.

Seasonal restrictions on sales of fresh and frozen game were under review as this cook book went to print. For the latest information consult The Countryside Alliance's website, www.gametoeat.co.uk.

Game seasons

A brief guide for chefs and cooks who want their game fresh rather than frozen

Pheasant	Oct 1 to Feb 1 (to Jan 31 in Northern Ireland)
Partridge	Sept 1 to Feb 1 (to Jan 31 in Northern Ireland)
Red Grouse	Aug 12 to Dec 10 (to Nov 30 in Northern Ireland)
Common Snipe	Aug 12 to Jan 31 (Sept 1 to Jan 31 in Northern Ireland)
Woodcock	Oct 1 to Jan 31 (Sept 1 to Jan 31 in Scotland)
Wild Geese & Duck	Sept 1 to Jan 31 (to Feb 20 on the foreshore)
Woodpigeon	No close season
Rabbit	No close season
Hare	No close season (cannot be sold March through July)

Deer

Red and Sika (stags)	Aug 1 to Apr 30	(July 1 to Oct 20 in Scotland)
Red and Sika (hinds)	Nov 1 to Feb 28/29	(Oct 21 to Feb 15 in Scotland)
Fallow (bucks)	Aug 1 to Apr 30	
Fallow (does)	Nov 1 to Feb 28/9	(Oct 21 to Feb 15 in Scotland)
Roe (bucks)	Apr 1 to Oct 31	(Apr 1 to Oct 20 in Scotland)
Roe (does)	Nov 1 to Feb 28/9	(Oct 21 to Mar 31 in Scotland)
Muntjac	No close season	
Chinese Water Deer	No close season	

Details of regional variations and seasons for other species are available via the Countryside Alliance website, http://www.countryside-alliance.org.uk.

Conversions

Oven Temperatures

°C	°F	Gas Mark	Oven
140	275	1	Cool
150	300	2	
170	325	3	Moderate
180	350	4	
190	375	5	Moderately Hot
200	400	6	
220	425	7	Hot
230	450	8	
240	475	9	Very Hot

Liquid Measurements

5ml	1 teaspoon (tsp)
10ml	1 dessertspoon (dsp)
15ml	1 tablespoon (tbsp) or 1/2 fl oz
30ml	1 fl oz
60ml	2 fl oz
75ml	2 1/2 fl oz
100ml	3 1/2 fl oz
150ml	5 fl oz (1/4 pt)
300ml	1/2 pt
450ml	3/4 pt
600ml	1 pt (20 fl oz)
1 litre	1 3/4 pt

Weights

15g	1/2 oz
25g	1 oz
50g	2 oz
75g	3 oz
110g	4 oz (1/4lb)
150g	5 oz
175g	6 oz
200g	7 oz
225g	8 oz (1/2lb)
250g	9 oz
275g	10 oz
300g	11 oz
350g	12 oz (3/4 lb)
375g	13 oz
400g	14 oz
425g	15 oz
450g	16 oz (1lb)
500g	1lb 2 oz
675g	22 oz (1 1/2lb)
1kg	2.2lb

All conversions
are approximate

Wine

Choosing wines to drink with game is largely a matter of personal preference; there are no hard and fast rules. From the wide variety of wines from Europe and the New World, our chefs and their wine suppliers recommend the following as a general guide:

Gamebirds
Red Burgundy, Rioja, New World Pinot Noir and Cabernet Sauvignon, red Bordeaux, Côtes du Rhône reds

Duck and Goose
Red Bordeaux, red Burgundy, Côtes du Rhône, New World Syrah, Shiraz and Merlot, South African Pinotage, also Riesling and other full whites

Venison and Hare
Red Bordeaux, red Burgundy, Côtes du Rhône, New World Syrah, Shiraz, Zinfandel and Merlot, South African Pinotage, Chianti

game-to-eat

Useful information

Looking for a game dealer or a restaurant that serves game near you?

Apart from consulting the Yellow Pages or asking a friend who goes shooting, the best way of finding out is to check on the internet. A good starting point is The Countryside Alliance's Game-to-Eat website at www.gametoeat.co.uk

For more information, contact:

Game-to-Eat
8 High Street
Hurstpierpoint
West Sussex BN6 9TY
Tel 01273 834716
Email jane@fml-pr.co.uk

Yorkshire Game
Station Road Industrial Park
Brompton on Swale
Richmond
N Yorks DL10 7SN
Tel 01748 810212
www.yorkshiregame.co.uk

Rick Bestwick Ltd
Park Road
Holmewood Industrial Park
Chesterfield S42 5UY
Tel 01246 854999
www.rickbestwick.com

The UK Game Company
The Game Factory
West Marsh Road
Spalding
Lincs PE11 2BB
Tel 01775 710810
Email ukgame@hotmail.com

Notes